The Church
We Yearn For

To the search committee,
Community Unitarian.
with best wishes,

Michael Durall
—

OTHER BOOKS BY MICHAEL DURALL

Creating Congregations of Generous People

Beyond the Collection Plate

The Almost Church

Living a Call: Ministers and Congregations Together

The Almost Church Revitalized

Church Do's and Don'ts: Tips for Success, Pitfalls to Avoid

The Church
We Yearn For

The Search for a New Minister as a Revolutionary Event
in the Life and Times of Your Congregation

Michael Durall

COMMONWEALTH

MICHAEL DURALL

The Church We Yearn For

The Search for a New Minister as a Revolutionary Event
in the Life and Times of Your Congregation

Published by CommonWealth Consulting Group
900 Washington Street, Suite 303
Denver, CO 80203
www.vitalcongregations.com

Copyright © 2012 by Michael Durall

ISBN 978-1-4675-2595-4

Printed in the United States of America

CONTENTS

To my sons, Graham and Drew,
who give me hope for the future.

Search committees are not in the hiring business.
They are in the church transformation business.
— Loren Mead

There comes a time in the life of the church
when codes and customs, values and virtues, even words and symbols
become worn and jaded. They seem to lose much of their efficacy
and no longer command any authority in people's lives.
— Kortright Davis

Acknowledgements

I would like to thank many kind souls who contributed to this book. They include: Douglas Anders, Sara Ascher, Meg Barnhouse, David Blanchard, Lou Blanchard, David R. Boone, Jeff Bradley, Ginny Brown Daniel, San Daugherty, Betty Lynn Ferguson, Dorothy Lester, Jane Mar, Jim Matera, Kevin McLemore, Bob Middleton, Holly Miller-Shank, Anthony Pappas, Fred Pardee, Priscilla Richter, and Sherri Taylor.

A Revolutionary Approach

This book is based on three powerful ideas. The first is a comment by the writer Paul Wilkes, who said, "Churches should be called to do things they think they cannot do."

The second is the conviction of countless financial planners that middle-class Americans could double their charitable giving to all causes and not notice the slightest difference in their day-to-day lives. This means your church could double its annual pledge drive with ease. Isn't it breathtaking to imagine how many opportunities for expanded ministry this would open up for your church?

The third is that few congregations have an inkling of their true potential. Let me provide a few examples. An Episcopal church of 65 members in a hardscrabble mountain town in Colorado, through a combination of volunteers, food suppliers, and financial donors, serves 2,500 meals each month to local residents. Even with its small size, this church has a profound reason for being, one that truly reflects the presence of a living God.

If your church doubled its annual pledge drive, you could start, or substantially fund, a walk-in health clinic or a legal aid office in a marginal neighborhood. Think of the thousands of lives that would be made better, thanks to your congregation.

But there's no need to think small. A Congregational church in Connecticut raised money, pulled some strings around town, and built a Boys and Girls Club. These examples are within the grasp of most congregations across the land; if not alone, then in partnership with other churches in your region.

This book is full of hope for the future. I'm optimistic because I believe people of faith, clergy and lay alike, are increasingly dissatisfied with churches that are inward focused, live out the same year over and again, and do little to create a more just and humane world.

I also believe clergy, lay leaders, and people in the pews are tired of standing on the sidelines while others claim center stage—voices that preach intolerance, rage, and resentment. And, I believe American churchgoers are disturbed by their congregations remaining on membership plateaus while increasing numbers of people are lost and lonely; lost in their electronic worlds as surely as they are in the real world around them.

I've heard too many church members say, "When we encounter sorrow and injustice in the world, we feel so helpless." Surely, a feeling of helplessness cannot be the culmination of our lives together in religious community.

I've also heard parishioners say, "Well, everyone is so busy, no one has time for anything like that." I don't believe this for a minute. The average American now spends 50 hours per week or more involved with some type of electronic media. That's seven hours each day. People find time for things that are important.

This book asserts that we are capable of creating compelling ministries that convey to others, "Come join us in a cause that is larger than yourself, in a life-transforming community of faith." This is, indeed, the church we yearn for. But this church will require stronger leadership than we have seen in the past, clergy and lay alike. This church will also require people in the pews to completely re-think what the role and purpose of their congregation actually is.

Many books about congregational life present engaging scenarios for the future, but we need to consider another essential factor:

> *The catalyst for systemic change may emanate from search committees, and the ministers they select. This is vastly more controversial than it appears, because numerous studies have concluded, "Rarely do search committees claim they want a minister who will lead the congregation in new and innovative directions.*[1]

If a search committee selects a personable, middle-of-the-road pastor, it may be many years before that church has another chance to find far-sighted clergy leadership and live out its genuine call to ministry. In the meantime, long-established patterns of congregational life, many of which are the root causes of decline in the first place, become even more entrenched.

I hope my perspective will be an eye-opener to people who embark upon the holy work of the search for a new minister. In general, most search committees view their role as finding an acceptable minister who will be well liked by church members. Thus, congregational life continues as before. This is what parishioners claim they want, but this is not what search committees should do.

I believe the search for compliant ministers is a primary reason why mainline Protestantism is faltering in America today.

Today, the majority of Protestant churches are small or mid-sized, and few seek robust ministerial leadership. Most churches, if not in conflict, are comfortable with who they are. They search for ministers who will blend in. Too much of the search literature implies that ministerial candidates should accept congregations as they find them, and not challenge ineffective customs and ways. Some tweaks perhaps, but little more. Certainly nothing drastic.

As a parish consultant, the most difficult congregations I've ever worked with were the most comfortably settled in. I've actually heard church members say the pastor's role is to keep members happy, to make them feel good. How in the world have we regressed from the power of the Gospel to churches that function like social clubs?

The life of Jesus was certainly not about comfort and feeling good. For the past 2,000 years or so, the most effective ministers have been those who pushed boundaries, took risks, and led their congregations into uncharted territory. These are congregations that will not settle for comfort or mediocrity in what they do. That's why I'm optimistic about the future of the church.

Being comforted and feeling good? That's what restaurants, coffee shops, and spas are supposed to do. If that's all the church has to offer, no wonder people have left in large numbers. It's time to consider some startling alternatives.

CHAPTER 1

Let's Start at the Beginning

"Being a minister in search is not having interviews.
It's laying your life on the line."
— UCC minister Jonathan Clark

Nominees to the United States Supreme Court and ministers looking for new churches might share something in common. They are among the most highly scrutinized job seekers in the land. Supreme Court justices may actually have it easier. Once confirmed by the Senate, they aren't accountable to anyone who voted them in.

The search for a new minister can be a smooth path, a rocky road, or a combination of the two. Good intentions abound. But search committees and ministerial candidates beginning this journey can't predict with any certainty which route they will travel. All concerned hope to have a straightforward time of it.

Paul advised the church in Corinth, "That all things should be done decently and in order." (1 Corinthians 14:40) But decency and order are unlikely, and quite possibly undesirable characteristics of the search process. As we will soon discover, the search for a new minister can yield many revelations. Some will be delightful, others less so.

To help make the search process less of an arduous task, this book compares, contrasts, and challenges ministerial search methods in mainline Protestant denominations. It also contains some tricks of the trade, along with a wide array of stories, anecdotes, words of wisdom, folklore, myths, and things that go bump in the night. Some are entertainingly funny, others achingly sad.

I've discovered that denominational entities tend to devise their own search guidelines independently of one another. Few in one denomination are knowledgeable about methods used by the others. This is unfortunate, as variations in the search process from one denomination to another are definitely worth noting.

One of my goals in this book is to create better-informed search committees and ministerial candidates alike. There's no reason to reinvent wheels, or lack insight into how others conduct the task.

However, many books and denominational guidelines on the subject of ministerial search are relatively similar. They focus on the process itself. Form a committee, conduct a congregational survey, set deadlines, interview candidates, and in the end, a successful match is made.

I'm not suggesting these books and denominational materials are unhelpful. They provide excellent advice, include useful guidelines and checklists, and propose thoughtful questions that ministers and congregations alike should take into account. But Baptist minister Anthony Pappas writes, "Without passion, what good are our practices and procedures?"[1]

Pappas's comment brings us back to the main point of this book. A more compelling call to ministry is not contained in the instructions, guidelines, and checklists alone. For example, anyone who has assembled a child's swing set knows that the instructions don't convey the whole story. Those nuts and bolts don't always line up where they are supposed to, not to mention a missing piece or two.

> *Nor do the instructions ever suggest that you could reassemble all those pieces and make something completely different.*

I'm also not suggesting that the traditional search method is ineffective. Quite the contrary, I endorse the advice offered in many books to "trust the process." When churches claim they are "unique" and devise their own approaches, they risk making inferior or disastrous choices. What I am suggesting is that search committees and congregations alike expand their thinking about what a more engaging ministry looks like in this place and time.

This book does not replicate the step-by-step details of the search process, as these are readily available from denominational sources. Rather, I'll provide a behind-the-scenes view, taking into account the human drama in which search committees and candidates find themselves swept along.

A bad ministerial placement is almost always a mutual mistake, with both the search committee and the minister sharing the blame. Thus, a clearer understanding of the search process, from both the search committee's point of view and the minister's point of view, can greatly expand the potential for successful ministry.

With greater potential in mind, we might recall Isaiah, 43:18-19, "Remember not the former things, neither consider the things of old. Behold, I will show you a new thing. Now it will spring forth, shall you not know it? I will even make a way in the wilderness, and rivers in the desert."

If you and your fellow search committee members are thirsty for the living water of authentic ministry, and if your congregation has wandered in the desert of mediocrity long enough, read on.

CHAPTER 2

Sizing Up the Ministerial Candidate

*"I am constantly amazed at how many search committee members
have no clue what a minister does."*
—A Denominational Settlement Representative

I f you've found yourself on a search committee, no doubt you understand the need to set some ground rules and figure out how the
committee is going to conduct its business. At the same time, I suspect
you're intensely curious about ministerial candidates you'll be interviewing later on. After all, that's the whole purpose of a search committee.

So let's cut to the chase and add the perspective of the minister in
search. This may appear to be putting the end before the beginning, but
it's vitally important for search committees to comprehend the minister's
point of view early on. Subsequent chapters address policies, procedures,
and other extremely important things you'll need to know.

I'd like to tell you an "everywoman" tale about a minister in search.
We'll follow her through periods of joy and happiness, doubt and
uncertainty, and see how she fares in the end. I hope this little story
will help search committees understand what has brought a particular
candidate to your doorstep.

The Minister in Search

Pastor Sarah Clifton was shown into the conference room by the chair
of the search committee, where the other members of the committee
milled about. She introduced herself around the room. The search
committee noted her quiet, confident manner. Compared to other ministers they had interviewed, a few committee members felt instinctively that
she was the ideal choice.

However, ministers often claim that search committees focus on the wrong characteristics. Search committees are accused of being swayed by personality, appearance, poise, and charisma, rather than discerning the inner nature of the person.[1] Sometimes, a type of romantic infatuation allows each side to see only lovely possibilities and not stark realties in the other. This is human nature.

But 1 Samuel 16:7, says, "Man looks at the outward appearance, but the Lord looks at the heart." There's also the issue that the most qualified candidate doesn't always get the job, but rather the one who interviews most effectively.

Of course, interviews are a two-way street, and some ministers believe in their own invulnerability. As in, there's nothing wrong with this church that a good minister like me couldn't fix. The previous five ministers may have fallen short, but surely I'll turn this place around.[2]

Beneath the surface

Pastor Clifton's composure didn't come all that easily. She was in her ninth year as the sole minister of her current congregation, her first settlement, and by all outward measures had been successful. The congregation had grown slightly over the years, weathered a few storms, and Sarah was the beneficiary of a great deal of good will from congregants for her work.

However, at the six-year mark, Sarah began to wonder if she had accomplished everything there was to accomplish. She decided to update her ministry profile, a type of resume that ministers in mainline denominations employ. Instinctively, she knew it was better to leave when things were going well rather than stay too long. And, she was beginning to think it might be time for someone else to lead the congregation in new directions. But upon getting the forms, she was wracked with guilt at the thought of breaking the covenant she had established with her current congregation.

She was deeply concerned about remaining authentic to her parishioners while in search. Surely, they would know if she was tuning out. She also realized that looking for a new church is inordinately time-consuming, and each hour spent exploring her options would take away an hour from parish work. Keeping a secret from her parishioners was also unnerving. She put the ministerial profile forms in her desk, where they remained untouched for two years.[3]

During those two years, Sarah became convinced that she was not going to realize her long-term goals in ministry with this congregation, and that God was calling her to something beyond. She filled out the forms and notified her denominational offices that she was in search.

Because of her solid reputation, Sarah received inquires from a number of churches; a church near the ocean in Southern California, a white-steeple church in New England, a progressive church in the Midwest. A number of other congregations contacted her as well. Each had its particular appeal. Sarah and her husband invested an inordinate amount of time envisioning themselves in each setting. It was time-consuming and extremely distracting to her daily work.

Sarah forwarded her ministerial profile to three churches, confident that she would have numerous alternatives. Some weeks later, she received e-mail from her two top choices, informing her that she was not selected to interview. She was rattled. Beyond her disappointment, it dawned on her how competitive the search might be. She didn't even make the first cut!

Thankfully, she was not in a state of anxiety to move, as were some of her colleagues. Ministers in desperation sometimes move to churches in desperation, red flags and all, just to get out of town and start anew somewhere else. She knew that many of these ministries subsequently failed. She couldn't imagine doing that.

Sarah received an inquiry from the third church, and following a number of telephone conversations, was asked to interview. She did her homework, spent a great deal of time reviewing the church's profile, and got on a plane. Her weekend with the search committee was both exhilarating and draining. She thought she did well in addressing the search committee's questions and concerns.

A few days later, she was informed that she was not chosen as the candidate. All of a sudden, the task of being in search appeared overwhelming. She couldn't envision investing the time, emotional energy, and travel, for another year, perhaps longer.

Sarah struggled to maintain a professional appearance. Was she to continue this charade with her congregation? Plus, she realized her search was at the mercy of churches that would become available in a one-year or two-year timeframe. It's not like she could apply anywhere and anytime she wanted, like secular jobs.

You never know what will happen next

Most ministers, in fact, do interview with a number of churches before finding a match. Like all job seekers, not getting a job offer can be a blow to a minister's self-esteem. What more could this church possibly want? Some ministers also claim that by the time they visited, if they were the third of three candidates, the search committee had chosen a minister and was just going through the motions.

Later on, when ministers discover who the competition was, they sometimes react in disbelief. "Old First Church selected him?" Envy is on the sinful side of the ledger, but after all, ministers are human, too. But still, how could Old First Church have made such a choice?

Sarah received an inquiry from a congregation that was not on her list, with whom she was now interviewing. She thought this might be a nudge from the Holy Spirit. This congregation's profile reflected a great deal of thought. Her discreet inquiries revealed the church got high marks. The search committee chair was very gracious on the phone. So here she was.

She answered the obligatory questions about her call to ministry and why she was looking to move. She felt too many questions could be addressed with her pre-rehearsed answers, and wished the committee had been more specific about their vision for the future.

In turn, she asked the search committee a range of requisite though important questions about what was going on in the church. Samples of such questions are contained in all denominational search literature.

Sarah also asked the search committee probing questions about how much authority she would hold as minister, and who really wielded power in the congregation. She brought up one of her favorite subjects, "the sacred cow roundup" to find out what traditions might be inviolate. She also inquired about what a new minister might do to get in big trouble. She minced no words and got to the point.

She was impressed that committee members had read her portfolio carefully. They were genuinely interested in her. They were also some light-hearted moments, which Sarah took as a good sign. This reminded her of a colleague who said of the church that eventually called him, "I thought I could have fun with these people."

Under the surface

As candid as Sarah was in answering the committee's questions, she had not told the whole story about her own spiritual journey. Sarah had perceived a call to ministry at an early age, and had pursued it ever since. In seminary, her fellow students perceived her as dedicated and hard working. None of her professors had served as parish ministers, though, and there was little talk about the minister's role in a congregational setting during the three years she was a student.

She recalled an anecdote about a seminary dean who, some decades before, was asked whether the school should impart a sound theological education, or skills in practical ministry. The dean came down heavily on the side of theological education, adding, "Now our ministers might go out there and ruin a church or two, but they eventually learn."

Sarah also heard through the grapevine that some churches merely want the minister to be a hired hand, to marry them and bury them. Longer-term members ran the church and resented the minister's input. She shuddered at the thought.

She had taken a couple of one-day seminars about church leadership, but had questioned the assumption that various methods apply to both large and small congregations. However, she was grateful for some leadership insights she had gained, especially resistance to new ideas. One article by a newly settled minister was especially discerning, and included this anecdote:

> *Week after week, I exhorted the congregation to embrace risk and change. As one proposal after another hit the wall of their vast and impenetrable indifference, I found myself in a soul-crushing loop. Some new idea would fill me with fresh enthusiasm and renewed energy, followed by frustration and anger as the congregation schooled me in the inexorable law of Leadership 101: you can't lead if no one is following. I blamed myself; and yes, I blamed them.*[4]

Another seminar included a glimpse into leadership from a secular perspective, and focused on why good ideas that are generated by well-intentioned, talented people often fail. Sarah realized a fallacy in her own thinking, that if she presented good ideas in clear and logical ways, reasonable people would agree.

A related article pointed out that introducing new ideas meant introducing them to human beings, who have anxieties, contrary opinions, and a constant fear of what a new idea might do to their standing in the group. Added to this was a basic skepticism about new ideas in general.[5]

This article also articulated many common ways people react negatively or indifferently to new ideas, including:

Why change?
We don't have the money
You exaggerate the problem
Are you implying we're now wrong?
What's the hidden agenda?
No one else does this
Are you abandoning our core values?
We already have too many concerns
We've tried that before
This is too difficult to understand
Good idea, bad timing
Too much work
Won't work here, we're different
We're not ready for something like that
Puts us on a slippery slope
You'll never convince enough people
We're not equipped to do something like that

Sarah had read that all too often, the established culture of a congregation changes the leader, rather than the minister changing the congregation. She didn't view herself as a natural leader, wasn't sure what church leadership actually involved, or if she had the skills to lead a parish.

Sarah's internship was in a multi-staff church, and the senior minister believed she should be introduced to liturgy, worship planning, and how to conduct weddings and memorial services. This turned out to be excellent experience, but she was provided little exposure to church management, budgeting, administration, and finance.

When Sarah interviewed with the church she currently served, she was naïve about the parish minister's actual range of responsibilities. But her dedication to ministry carried the day. She was thrilled to be called to her first church, but in the back of her mind she was thinking, "What do I do now?"

Of course, Sarah wanted to do well in her first ministry. But she also had some hesitations. She had heard that church programs were mostly determined by which volunteers wished to be leaders, and that program quality was inconsistent at best and sometimes very poor. Some programs were repeated year after year, and led by the same church members.

She also realized that church calendars were often cluttered with programs and events, which was good in itself, but all this activity had no particular sequence, direction, or larger purpose. There was no clear beginning and no clear end, but rather a selection of random programs that didn't seem to contribute to the sense of what the congregation as a whole was called to become.[6]

She also remembered hearing that the traditional committee structure implemented decades ago remained intact in many congregations, whether effective or not.

Surprise!

The very first day on her first job as a pastor was quite memorable. It began with a staff member of 20 years standing, who was cordial when she met him during her interviews, hinting strongly that he would broach no meddling from her. Sarah realized that confronting a seasoned staffer would be suicidal. This put an immediate damper on some new ideas she had in mind.

Three weeks later, the other half-time staffer announced that she was planning a six-month sabbatical, even though her contract didn't contain a sabbatical provision. This staff person had floated the idea among a number of influential congregants, who thought it had merit. This put the board in the position of being spoilsports, and the chairman asked for Sarah's advice. If she disapproved the request, she'd have a disgruntled employee on her hands. If she approved the request, there would be a huge gap in a significant church program that could not easily be filled. A lose-lose situation if there ever was one.

Sarah knew the annual pledge drive had struggled to make its goal, but didn't realize how many limitations a financial shortfall would impose on her ministry. There was so little money to try anything new. Thankfully, a respected member of the church stepped forward and offered to lead the drive for the next two years. She prayed that an improved financial situation would be more beneficial to her ministry and the congregation.

Sarah's church board was useful, but didn't grasp the challenges she faced. It felt like her call to ministry, and the congregation's call as well, were ambiguous at best. The church's vision statement was rambling and vague, and had not been reviewed for years. Few in the church even knew what it was.

When she introduced new ministry possibilities to board members, the reaction was either to think about if further, or, "Keep us informed how that plays out." Sarah wondered if she should be more skilled at recruiting volunteers and delegating tasks.

A few months into her ministry, three members of the board rotated off and three new ones appeared. A new learning curve began and many conversations felt repetitious. Two of the most recently appointed board members had served ten years before, and she felt they wanted to take the church back in time. One of them had the potential to become a severe critic.

Hanging in there

Sarah proved to be a resilient soul. As the years went by, she came to care for her congregation very much. In return, they exhibited a genuine love of her. They arranged a very nice fifth anniversary celebration for her, and she was very touched. All things considered, she was proud of what she and her congregation had accomplished.

But she also deeply troubled. Sarah believed that church, religion, and matters of faith were minor adjuncts to her congregants' lives, rather than a way of life. A colleague of hers had commented, "Our faith is the dessert on our full plates, not the organizing principle of our lives."[7]

Sarah felt that a life of faith meant that we examine and change the way we relate to the secular world. She believed fervently that people of faith should give themselves over to a larger cause, even if that meant making sacrifices. She felt this was the heart and soul of the religious life, but sacrifice was not what her congregants wanted to hear. She berated herself for lacking the courage to challenge her congregants' established way of life, and believed her ministry was diminished in this regard.

Sarah was also disturbed by the Gospels not confronting the prevailing consumer culture, but being compromised by it. Many of her congregants, in this relatively affluent community, led the proverbial good life. They bought expensive homes, vacation homes, and pricey cars. They sent their kids to private schools. They traveled abroad.

She was invited to open houses, during which church members showed off costly new kitchens and master bedroom spas. Sarah maintained a convivial presence at these events, but seethed inside at the inability of this congregation to be more generous financially, and the lack of mission programs that helped those who were less fortunate. Slate floors shipped in from India for the kitchen! Was this necessary?

At times, Sarah felt like a passenger on a bus that was already in motion, and she was not in the driver's seat. She wasn't sure who the driver was. She also felt her job was like circus performers she had seen as a child, who spin plates on long, thin rods. Once the plates began spinning, the performer had to dash back to each plate repeatedly, to keep them up to speed.

She didn't view her ministry as leadership at all. Rather, she seemed to be incessantly running back and forth, rescuing those plates at the last second, hoping they wouldn't fall and crash to the floor. She was also distressed at some of the attitudes of church members. Too many of her congregants' image of themselves had to do with being served rather than being called to serve.

She was upset that numerous parents, after registering their children for Sunday school, dropped off their kids on Sunday mornings and picked them up later. Some of these parents were non-members. They viewed the church as free childcare. She was also disheartened by the complaints from Sunday school teachers, who told her that many parents hadn't introduced themselves and didn't stop by the classroom to see how their children were doing.

Sarah was also angry when she spent a great deal of time with a young couple, preparing for their child's baptism. Following the baptism ceremony on a Sunday morning, Sarah never saw them again. Three months later, she learned the couple had joined another church a few miles down the road.

Sarah felt the baptism incident was an extension of church members making up their own rules about their participation and commitment, rather than the church setting standards. But this was an issue that few in the leadership wanted to discuss.

Sarah's strong suit was liturgy, worship, and preaching. She prepared every detail thoroughly, practiced her sermon delivery carefully, and was confident going into the pulpit on Sunday mornings. From her parishioners' point of view, Sarah had the situation well in hand. She had the congregation's respect and admiration, but all too often she felt like the Wizard of Oz, behind the screen manipulating the levers.

Behind that screen

The secret that Sarah kept from the search committee, and from her congregants back home, is that she routinely worked 65 hours a week, sometimes more, to keep everything in a reasonable balance. Her supposed day off was a myth. When someone in the congregation passed away and a memorial service was scheduled, this added ten to fifteen hours to her workweek. In the past year, she had conducted eighteen funerals.

She attended committee meetings during evening hours, and was available whenever parishioners needed her. She feared she had become a minister who "needed to be needed," and was involved in almost every aspect of congregational life. She also accepted a volunteer role with the denomination to increase her visibility beyond the local parish, which sometimes involved travel to other cities.

In the early years, her husband had been enrolled in a demanding graduate program and they didn't have children, so Sarah didn't worry about her intense work schedule. But now, she didn't know how to cut back, and felt guilty even thinking about it. She had raised the level of expectations extremely high, and thought her congregants would surely notice if she was less accessible. She was exhausted.

Since her husband had completed his graduate degree, he was beginning to complain about her absence from the home. She recognized herself in a book written by Episcopal minister Barbara Brown Taylor, who wrote,

> *My tiredness was so deep that it had seeped into my bones. I was out more nights than I was home. No matter how many day planners I bought, none of them told me when I had done enough. By the time I got home at night, it was all I could do to pay the bills and go to bed. I pecked God on the cheek the same way I did my husband, drying up inside for want of making love.*[8]

Sarah knew too many colleagues who were divorced because the church had become "the other man," or "the other woman." She had come to understand the sad irony all too well, that parish ministry is a grueling and not a family-friendly occupation.

She also felt her biological clock ticking, and wanted to start a family. But she was interviewing with a larger congregation that might hold out even more demands than she was facing now. Her husband told her that many female ministers have learned to balance both careers and families. But she remained unconvinced, and wondered if she was bearing false witness to the search committee.

Despite her uncertainty, part of her thought that because she was successful in one ministry, she would be successful in the next. She had a good track record. This was the primary reason the search committee was interested in her. She would make it happen through stamina and force of will. Was she being honest with this search committee, or was she going through mental gyrations to make everything fit?

In her most soul-searching moments, she wondered if she was complicit in creating such a stressful situation for herself in her current church. She realized that she was. If called to this new church, would she be exchanging one set of spinning plates for another?

At the same time, she couldn't imagine doing any other kind of work. Ministry was her life; there was no other. But she had also read a number of books about envisioning an entire new way of congregational life, and was highly intrigued. At times, Sarah felt like this was not the search for another parish, but the search for her own soul.

She'd seen a new congregation start from scratch just down the road from her current church, and in a short time, had grown in size significantly. The liturgy and music and outreach were all new and exciting. She felt a calling to serve such a church, even though she'd never done this kind of ministry and didn't know if she had the skill or talent to succeed. She knew the qualifications included:

That faith is the foundation for everything in life

An attraction toward people on the edge of conventional church circles, and possibly beyond

A clear and amazingly simple sense of mission. (Two that Sarah particularly liked were, "You will be cared for, and will be called upon to care for others." And, "Every member a ministry.")

The passionate conviction that the church offers something that will renew human lives and communities

The belief that God sent us to this particular place in this particular moment for a particular reason

A keen awareness of the ways that organized religion has fallen short of living out the Christian good news faithfully and effectively

A determination to clear some new territory – to push the church to new places and to new people

Boredom with unchanging routine and maintenance tasks

A sense of urgency rather than complacency, characterized by energy toward immediate, short-term goals

The capacity to communicate our spiritual experience and vision winsomely to others, so they are persuaded to jump aboard the bandwagon[9]

This type of ministry made Sarah's heart sing, but would the church she was interviewing with remotely consider such far-reaching ideas? She wasn't sure whether to broach the subject or not.

Part of her thought she should tell the search committee what they wanted to hear, but part of her wanted to tell the search committee all of the above. She liked these people very much, but did they wish to preserve the current-day church forevermore? Maybe they were tired of the familiar routine, as well.

Should she play it safe, increasing her chances of getting a new settlement? Or should she bare her soul and tell all, with the risk that this church would pass her by, for a minister more in the mainstream?

What's a minister to do?

Readers expecting a definitive answer to Sarah's dilemma will not find one here. This is the nature and character of the search process. If you were Sarah, what would you do?

If you were a member of the search committee and Sarah proposed ideas like changing the time of the Sunday service, the music, the expectations of membership, the amount of money people were expected to give, a 50 percent increase in outreach, a second worship service in Spanish, a partnership with an African American church, and a mission in a foreign country, would you think you had found an inspirational leader? Or would Sarah's candidacy be doomed?

My goal in this chapter is twofold. First, to shine some light on the life of a typical pastor, because congregations all too often underestimate the complexity of parish ministry. A significant skill set is required for church leadership, one that takes years to develop. All too often, the low pay and spiritual dimensions of the work lull search committees and congregants alike into a false belief that what is primarily required is good intentions and hard work.[10]

The second is to note that some churches are clergy healing, and some are clergy draining. I hope your church understands the difference, and opts for the former. My hope, dream, and prayer for your congregation is that you select a pastor who has a strong, visible, and powerful call to ministry. In turn, your congregation will share that call, and embark upon a journey of faith for all.

I once visited a congregation that had a unique letterhead stationery. The name of the church, address, and phone number were not at the top of the page, but at the bottom. At the top was an appealing graphic image, accompanied by the phrase, "The adventure of a lifetime begins here." The minister, lay leaders, and church members believed this to be true, and created a congregation in this image and likeness.

Your congregation should do no less.

CHAPTER 3

Does Your Church Have a Soul?

*"When I first arrived, I had lost everything –
my husband, my job, my health. This church saved my life."*
—A grateful parishioner offering thanks

I'd like to begin by recounting a phone conversation with a search committee chair about what his church would offer a new minister. He said the search committee had spent a great deal of time in prayer during the early stages, attempting to determine if the congregation could claim that it was a model employer.

When working with congregations, I often ask clergy and lay leaders if their churches have souls. I get answers ranging from a robust engine of a soul to a shriveled-up raisin of a soul. I hadn't equated a church being a model employer with having a particular kind of soul, but I believe this is an apt comparison.

A congregation-wide discussion about whether your church is a model employer, based on the issues listed below, will be a powerful method to determine the dimensions of your collective soul, what God is calling you to do, and the minister you are seeking.

The search committee in question realized the congregation fell short in numerous areas, but vowed they would help their new minister lead the congregation in becoming a center of ministry characterized by:

Lay leaders who believe they are actually leading the church somewhere, rather than serving as overseers of finance, administration, and committee work

A belief that the church should always be a place of respite for those who need it, but also a port of embarkation for new ministries that serve the world

Fiscal responsibility, but also a willingness to take some risks and not be bound by the debilitating tyranny of the operating budget – a constant reminder of all those things we cannot do

Awareness of the untapped giving potential of the congregation. It bears repeating that middle-class Americans could double their charitable giving to all causes, and notice little difference in their day-to-day lives. Most churches could double their annual pledges drive with ease

The funding of mission and outreach programs that equals or exceeds 10 percent of the operating budget

A music program that is not amateurish or "garage band" in nature

Continual efforts to achieve a well-functioning educational program for people of different generations

A well-maintained physical plant with preventive maintenance funds budgeted annually

Groups that attract members for study, prayer, and mission that are not closed to newcomers. Nothing communicates that new members are unwelcome more than closed groups

A culture of volunteers who feel empowered to initiate new ministries

A competent staff of non-clergy employees

Competitive compensation, with health and retirement benefits

Some readers, especially those in smaller congregations, may believe this church is beyond their grasp. Maybe so, but if you can't address all the above issues, try for a few. Making an attempt will appeal to the most dedicated and committed members of your congregation. Don't let naysayers consign your church to the past. And don't believe for a moment that the money isn't there. It most assuredly is.

I applaud the above description of a church because it indicates that congregants will stand by the minister in creating a church that strives to meet these standards. This is an antidote to the minister arriving on the scene and the congregational attitude being, "Well, I wonder what she'll do now?"

The search committee chairman I spoke with concluded by saying, "We desire to be a congregation that takes pride in who we are, how we serve the world, and are cognizant each and every day of the kind of people God is calling us to become." To me, this sums up just about everything that ministers and search committees need to discuss.

Are you willing to consider an alternative?

I'd like to add another perspective on what kind of church you might yearn to become, what type of soul is within reach. Noted author Lyle Schaller has defined two kinds of churches. The first is the church with European roots that functions like a voluntary association. In this church, members themselves determine the extent of their commitment and participation.

The second type of church is the community in covenant, more likely to be "made in America," in which the church sets the standards for membership. This church expects people to commit to the mission and work of the church before they are permitted to join.[1]

Of course, there are many variations in between, but the differences in these two approaches are significant and far-reaching. The principal difference is the expectations of membership.

I recommend churches not use the phrase "expectations of membership." Rather, I prefer "membership with integrity," or "membership in good standing." The word "expectations" can put people on guard and convey something they don't really want to do. Being a member in good standing is welcoming, inviting, and a goal to which people aspire. Who wants to be a member in poor standing?

The following is what membership in good standing should involve:

Attending Sunday worship regularly

Participating in one church program each year that deepens your faith

Being involved in a mission project beyond your church's four walls each year

Reaching the five to ten percent charitable giving level as soon as possible

Telling others about the church

Some readers may believe their church could never ask this much of its members, while others believe this is a low rung on the ladder. I'm with those who think these are minimal requirements.

Church leaders often believe that asking people for too much will drive them away. I believe that church members drift away because we ask too little. Today, people hunger to be part of something larger than themselves. Churches should offer this opportunity.

I've found that almost all problems a congregation encounters can be traced to low or ambiguous expectations of membership. Low expectations of membership is the albatross of mainline Protestantism. Nothing else makes a congregation inherently weaker, or stifles the awareness of God's presence.

But I have never seen a written church profile that indicated a willingness to raise member expectations. Nor have I found it in search literature.

The defining characteristic of low-expectation churches is that about 25 percent of members give most of the money and do most of the work. UCC minister Stephen Gray observes that the remaining 75 percent of members are "present" or relatively inert. This is a fundamental reason why half or more of the membership does not attend Sunday worship regularly.

In my view, the voluntary association church is inherently inequitable and ultimately unsustainable. Mainline Protestantism has fifty years of experience to attest to this fact.

I also believe the voluntary association church is a major reason why millions of Americans have left mainline Protestantism. Theologian Miroslav Volf claims that many churches do not fulfill their central task because they fail to offer a compelling vision of a way of life that is worth living.[2]

There's an old saying that Americans will do anything to lose weight except eat less and exercise more. It's the same with redefining the meaning of membership. In churches of many faith traditions, people claim they wish to grow the church, make it a stronger presence in the community, and expand its outreach programs. Few of these will occur in the low-expectation church.

Low expectations create a congregation in which the same problems occur repeatedly – difficulty in finding leaders, a constant struggle to recruit volunteers, volunteer burnout, tight budgets, and low-level pledging among two-thirds of the congregation, to name a familiar few.

Sadly, low-expectation attitudes are an established custom in tens of thousands of churches nationwide. These attitudes are fiercely resistant to change. Raising expectations is a "third rail" issue of church life. Touch it and risk immediate electrocution! Raising expectations is an issue that most congregants do not even want to think about.

A stunning alternative

So here's a rubber-meets-the-road issue for search committees and ministerial candidates alike, and the whole reason for this book. A low-expectation church is unlikely to be anything more in the future than it is today. Please pause a moment to consider the ramifications of what I have just claimed. For some readers, this may be good news. For others, it may be the most dreadful scenario imaginable.

If an extraordinarily engaging, forward-looking ministerial candidate asks the search committee if the congregation will reconsider the expectations of membership, what might the answer be? This is a question the search committee has probably not considered and does not how to answer. In addition, the search committee does not have the authority to decide what the expectations of membership should be.

In fact, some members of the search committee themselves might be opposed to redefining the meaning of membership.

> *This brings up the breathtaking issue of whether the dynamics between the search committee and the candidate outweigh the wishes put forth by congregants as to what kind of minister they seek. What if a candidate brought a compelling vision that most congregants, including the search committee, had never thought of?*

Most church profiles and search committees present a "this is who we are" perspective. It's not a hard line, take-it-or-leave-it attitude, but rather, the church is arranged the way congregants like it. In turn, few candidates may have the courage to inform the search committee that the congregation needs to be stood on its head to hear the voice of God, envision a new tomorrow, and live its true call to ministry.

I recall a Presbyterian minister who preached, "This church is not a finely-crafted vessel in which a small number of members labor down below, rowing, while a larger number of members take up residence in First Class, especially those who didn't buy a ticket to get on board. In this church, everyone takes a turn with the oars."

No successful organization functions on the basis of low expectations, or allows everyone to make up their own rules. Would you send your children to a school that claimed, "We don't expect much of our students." Would you allow your spouse to be admitted to a hospital that touted its lack of standards? Does any winning sports team have lax coaching? The idea is preposterous, yet this is how many churches function.

Churches should get out of the low-expectation business once and for all. This will require courageous ministers, search committees, and congregants alike.

Whatever the business or nonprofit organization, the best usually means people who take great pride in using their finest skills and talents to create something out of the ordinary. Don't you desire to be an integral part of creating one of the best churches in your community? Do you really want to spend your valuable religious life in a complacent church, in which each year is a replica of the one before? Is that truly the presence of the Holy Spirit among us?

Surprisingly, and counter-intuitively, raising the expectations of membership is also a key factor in growing a congregation numerically. People desire to be part of a community of meaning and purpose. This should be your goal, and is the very best form of evangelism available.

A brief note. The most effective way to introduce the topic of membership in good standing in your church is to start with new members coming in. Gradually, you will create a higher expectation environment. Older, more established members may not convert to the new ideal, but that's all right. Start where you can, and keep in mind that about 25 percent of your congregation already subscribes to the concept of membership in good standing. These hearty souls will be allies in the cause and would surely like some company.

Membership in good standing also requires a membership committee of stalwart souls who believe the church has changed their lives in some significant way, and who communicate the life-transforming power of their faith and service lived in and through the congregation. The membership committee is a powerful calling, not just another committee assignment. Make your church's membership committee a powerhouse.

I don't necessarily believe that introducing membership in good standing requires a vote of the board. If it does, and board members are reluctant, I urge supporters to challenge them about what is to be gained by maintaining a low-expectation environment. Bringing the issue to a congregational vote will result in a decision to scrap the entire idea. Avoid this at all cost.

Finally, when a search is underway, I urge people of good faith to gather together, pray together, ponder together, and listen for the voice of God in what your church's call to ministry might be. If you honestly seek out your congregation's reason for being, you will surely find it.

CHAPTER 4

The Greatest Peril of All

"They told me they wanted to change."
—A minister who was departing after eighteen months
because he took this comment at face value

C hurch guru Loren Mead once wrote that congregations sometimes view ministers like interchangeable light bulbs. If one burns out, just pop in another, turn the switch back on, and church continues as before.[1] I hasten to add that he does not endorse this view.

However, Mead's observation raises one of the most critical, least explored, and hazardous issues in the ministerial search process. That's whether a church actually wants to change, or if this often-stated desire is largely fictional. Three important issues need to be considered carefully in this discussion.

Things as they are

First, the status quo in congregational life has significant staying power. Churches of all sizes are akin to ships at sea. A sizable force is required to change direction, and even then, that ship might creak and groan mightily, resisting the force exerted. One observer noted that it takes seven miles to turn around an ocean liner, and seven years to change a church.

There's not a massive conspiracy in place to maintain things as they are. Rather, many congregants value the familiarity and predictability of church life. They pray together. They worship together and break bread together. They commemorate time-honored holy days and seasons of the church calendar. They look forward to seeing their fellow congregants on Sunday morning. They help those who are less fortunate. They celebrate together, and they mourn together. Congregations want to be loved, cared for, and lifted up. This is all very, very good.

People in the pews wouldn't come right out and say the church should never change. Some may think the church can change as long as they don't have to. But congregants tend to subscribe to the concept of gradualism, an honored belief that the best changes occur slowly. Church leaders frequently value the normal. Nothing too extreme!

These attitudes are among the reasons why well-educated, rational, intelligent adults can become hopping mad at even minor changes in the church, especially if they were not involved in making the decision.

Any seasoned churchgoer will recall heated discussions about changing the worship time from 9:45 to 10:00; slight changes in the music on Sunday morning; the new phone system; how chairs are arranged in the sanctuary; locked cabinets in the kitchen that mark turf battles; and why it's a waste of money to buy new choir robes when the old ones have been just fine for the past 30 years. Will the choir sing any better with new robes? Well then, what's the point?

Churches have many sacred cows. In the early 1800s, the debate was whether to install central heating in the building vs. parishioners continuing to bring coal boxes to heat their pews.

A small change can generate resentment vastly beyond the issue itself. This is especially the case when younger or newer members propose changes to the established order. An extra portion of antipathy can be directed toward the new minister "who doesn't know how we do things around here."

A newly-called minister told me that she concluded the Sunday service by facing the congregation, raising her arms and saying, "Go now in peace." This was a new ritual for the congregation. At coffee hour, a disgruntled congregant was heard to say, "Who does she think she is, telling us to go in peace!"

This brings to mind a gem of a book titled, *365 Ways to Criticize the Preacher.* Written in journal form, it's about a congregant's persistent hostility toward the new minister. One entry is, "The pastor and his wife took in a foster child. Is he a preacher or a social service agency?"[2]

Church members often believe they form a type of "social contract" with a minister. When that minister moves on, for whatever reason, people may feel that contract has been broken. They may not be ready to sign a new contract with a new minister just now. In fact, it might be quite a while before they recommit, if ever.[3]

Looking beyond the congregation's perspective

The second issue we need to address in regard to a congregation's willingness to change is the membership's scant awareness of American religion beyond their own four walls.

Many congregants are familiar only with the faith tradition in which they currently reside. Even if they've switched from one denomination to another, that new church is probably similar in liturgy and contains PLU, people like us. Not many Episcopalians become Pentecostals. This "in-house" perspective applies to the search committee, as well.

I'm not suggesting that loyalty to one's faith tradition is a bad thing. However, it creates a limited perspective. When looking toward the future, congregants and search committees alike are steeped in their own tradition. They envision the church of tomorrow as more or less comparable to the church of today.

Let's summarize briefly some changes that churches often wish to make. One of the most frequent desires is to grow numerically. Paradoxically, according to one church profile, they also wish to retain, "The intimate ambiance that has sustained us for so many years." These are incompatible goals. As churches grow in size, a defining factor is an increase in anonymity. Yet these incompatible beliefs persist.

Also on the wish list is the desire to be stronger in mission and outreach. Members would like to become more Biblically literate, or grow deeper in faith. Expansion of the Sunday school or the youth group would be a great boon, (even in a church that reported 77 percent of members were over 55 years of age, and none of them had children under 21 who attended church.) A new tenor and a couple of sopranos in the choir would be most excellent. The perennial hope exists that more members will take on volunteer roles and increase their charitable giving.

These claims are all well and good, and solidly grounded. But these hopes for the future exist within the congregation's current structures, guidelines, and conventions. If we add in the history of the denomination, these traditions might go back a couple of centuries. As one observer noted, many churches are like orchards planted 100 years ago. It's not easy to move those trees around.

Thus, most rank and file congregants have little concept of a church that could be markedly different from the one they know today. They tend to believe that new trees cannot be planted. Nor do congregants display much interest in exploring other possibilities because they are partial to what they have. People prefer the familiar to the unfamiliar.

Some denominations, and some congregations (who will remain nameless) also believe they do things the "right" way. What would another denomination offer that could possibly be of interest?

In addition, the proposed changes listed above are often phrased so they will not upset anyone, especially long-term members. The result is that too many churches function on a maintenance model, keeping the ship on an even keel and maintaining a steady course. This does not include sailing into uncharted waters.

This attitude is often reflected in church profiles that contain wording such as "we are highly educated, opinionated, and independent thinkers." Ministers take note. This actually means, "We have defined church on our own terms and do not wish for a new minister to tell us otherwise."

Personally, I believe maintaining the church as it is eventually becomes incredibly boring. That's why many people drift away. Thus, my challenge to congregations claiming they wish to change is "from what to what?" I often ask church leaders if systemic change will be required to envision a new future, or if minor tweaks will suffice. The vast majority of respondents answer that systemic change is necessary. They just don't know what that might include, nor do they realize the magnitude of adaptations that will be required to reach their stated goals.

A different kind of church

Allow me to provide a few examples of what the church of future looks like, because it's already here today.

A friend of mine, in her sixties and a fallen-way Lutheran since her youth, attended a Sunday worship service at a Vineyard Christian Fellowship, a fast-growing movement in America. She is cynical about religion, and I thought she would scoff at the rock and roll music and the informality of it all. Instead, she told me, "I cried. That service was designed to lead people into their pain. Once there, the remainder of the service led them out of that pain and gave them hope for the week ahead." I was stunned.

So another of my challenges to congregations, search committees, and ministerial candidates is to define the purpose of the Sunday worship service. I have to confess that I'd never thought about this until my friend told me of her experience. Now, I find it an issue of critical importance.

Next on the list of churches that don't fit the conventional mold, I recently attended Sunday services at a newly formed nondenominational church whose Christian theology would be quite familiar to Protestant churchgoers. An excellent, nine-piece band started off the service with some extraordinarily good music. If that band had played for an hour or so, I would have found it a perfectly acceptable worship experience.

Leading the band was a young man who sported a shaved head, a goatee that reached to mid-chest, and bare feet. The piano player wore a modified Mohawk haircut. The bass player was an African-American woman with dreadlocks reaching to her waist. The sanctuary was over-flowing with people whose average age was mid-twenties. It was a powerful experience.

And that's the point. Newly formed churches differ not in theology, but rather the vehicle in which that theology is delivered. These churches are based not only on "the word," as is the established church, but on "the experience" of a living God in people's lives.

Here's another example of what a new-definition of church looks like, a progressive, independent church near where I live. Parked at the entrance were half a dozen Harley Davidson motorcycles, with rough-looking owners taking a last toke on those cigarettes before coming inside. Once seated, I noticed a stocky young man in shorts, T-shirt, and a Yankees cap on backwards who was covered with tattoos from his neck to his feet. The front of his shirt read "Jesus loves my tattoos." In nonde-nominational churches, you see a lot of people you ordinarily wouldn't think go to church.

During the sermon, the minister said, "For a lot of you out there, life sucks, and it sucks big time. We have seven families in this church who will be evicted from their apartments at the end of the month, unless we help them today." When the collection plate came around, I threw in a couple of twenties. What else was I to do?

Newly formed churches often have a raw, gutsy, real-world trait about them - that life can be hard, very hard. But with God's help, and our being in community together, we can make those burdens lighter, for ourselves and for others.

A frequent message is, "We don't care who you are, where you've been, or what you've done. You're welcome here." Upon leaving that service, I felt I had participated in something important. UCC minister Anthony Robinson claims that too many churches behave as though nothing important is at stake. I hope your church doesn't fall into this category. Be honest with yourselves if it does.

A few more examples, then some advice

I live in Denver, Colorado, and two churches come immediately to mind. The first is Scum of the Earth Church, from a phrase in Ecclesiastes, founded by Presbyterian minister Mike Sares (www.scumoftheearth.net). This is a church for people who believe there isn't anywhere else they can go to church. Among the program offerings are "creating meaning out of entropy" and "writing Christian poetry that doesn't suck."

The second church is the House For All Saints and Sinners, founded by Lutheran minister/theologian Nadia Bolz-Weber (www.houseforall.org). This may be irrelevant, but she is over six feet tall, sports multiple tattoos, and is not exactly the stereotypical Lutheran pastor.

The House for All Saint and Sinners describes itself as, "A group of folks figuring out how to be a liturgical, Christo-centric, social-justice oriented, queer-inclusive, incarnational, contemplative, irreverent, ancient-future church with a progressive but deeply rooted theological imagination."

We might also include the Cowboy Christian Connection, an organization that helps unite some 700 interdenominational cowboy-specific ministries that have sprung up across the U.S. and Canada since the 1970s.[4]

Did I mention that church is a whole new ballgame out there?

One of my favorite churches is the fictional one in Anne Tyler's novel, *Saint Maybe*. The Church of the Second Chance is a place where people can find hope, healing, reconciliation, and atonement for deeds they once thought unforgivable.

All these churches do not even include the growing number of house churches, ministers who hold theological discussions in brewpubs at 10:00 pm on weeknights, or the rapidly growing online church that is open 24/7. All this is heady competition for the traditional church down at the corner of Main and Elm. How will your church define its future in such a rapidly changing environment?

Grown-ups, too

Lest readers think the church of the future is exclusively for the young, I recall a story told by Lyle Schaller. He spoke of a church that was in search for a new minister. The search committee did a very wise thing by visiting clergy and lay leaders of five or six other churches in the immediate vicinity, asking what the future might hold.

Each church's leadership replied that the future depended on families with young children. The church in search consisted mainly of middle-aged adults. The search committee realized it could not compete with these neighboring churches, and made the decision that mature adults would be their primary constituency and mission field. They agreed that the new minister would be a grandparent.

The church called a 55-year old grandfather, who said this church was the liveliest congregation he had ever served. The church purchased a reconditioned, long-distance bus, which made 40 trips per year; ranging in length from local, one-day trips to regional, three-day ventures. The minister said that bus produced seven or eight weddings each year, from lonely adults who had met on board.

This congregation of mature adults had time, money, expertise, and many were living second childhoods. They gave away large amounts of money to mission and outreach programs in the community. Like the old saying, youth may be wasted on the young. Don't think your future is limited when it may not be.

A bit of advice

I'm not suggesting that your church adopt any of the practices just mentioned, or attempt to become something it is not. I am suggesting that the written congregational profile that is presented to ministerial candidates, along with numerous ideas the congregation puts forward, are likely to reinforce established ways and not look to a future that is perceptively different.

Such profiles reflect an internal perspective based solely on members' views and opinions. Not taken into account are the seismic changes that have occurred in American religion and what this means for the mainline church.

If search committees, church leaders, and people in the pews wish to fully realize their congregation's inherent potential, they cannot

*accomplish this by sitting around a metaphorical conference table
inside the church building with only themselves as company.*

Search committee members need to go beyond their own four walls
and visit churches of other faiths, sizes, and approaches. These include large
nondenominational congregations, as well as "niche" churches that serve
small segments of society. The search committee should also invite lay leaders
to accompany them. This is eminently possible because many churches now
schedule services on Saturday and Sunday afternoons, and at mid-week.

You may not always like what you see, but visiting vividly different
churches will expand your horizon into what is possible for your congregation back home. Many good ideas arise from visiting churches of other
faiths. I find visiting other churches quite adventuresome, and believe
you will, too.

The real world out there

The third issue we need to discuss in regard to a congregation's willingness to change and what the future might hold is the external
environment in which churches exist today. Noted researcher George
Barna is an excellent guide. While there is always hope, mainline churches
face an array of mighty obstacles.

The following are a sample of Barna's findings, based on thousands of
surveys, personal interviews, and an analysis of extensive amounts of data.[5]

*Until the 1960s, mainline Protestantism was the heartbeat of
American Christianity. Today, the mainline has been renamed the
"sideline" by some, as traditional churches stagger from steady
losses in membership, attendance, income, and churches per capita.*

*In religious terms, one of the most dramatic shifts has been the
emergence of the "none" category as the fastest-growing group in
America.*

*It is increasingly common for people to shop and hop – to attend a
particular church, then switch allegiance to another church that
better suits their needs. Denominational loyalty has eroded substantially over the years.*

*One burgeoning segment of the Protestant community will continue
to be nondenominational and independent churches.*

Mainline churches have one of the lowest retention rates of their adherents from childhood through adulthood, about 44 percent; compared to Hindus (84 percent), Jews (76 percent), Orthodox Christians (73 percent), Mormons (70 percent), and Catholics (68 percent).

Overall confidence in churches and clergy has dropped to historic lows. Currently, less than half of the population gives clergy high marks for their honesty and ethical behavior.

Less than one out of five churches will increase their attendance in a given year; four out of five Protestant churches (80 percent) will remain on a plateau in membership or experience a reduction in adult attendance.

The median age of pastors is now fifty-four. In the last twenty years, the number of pastors under forty has decreased from 32 percent to 15 percent.

The median length of pastorate for a lead minister is six years. Pastors in mainline churches have an average tenure of only four years.

Barna's findings are all too familiar to clergy. One minister noted, "For those of us in parish ministry, it's just about impossible to get through our morning cornflakes without coming across yet one more study demonstrating the futility of our endeavors. We know the story all too well: aging and shrinking congregations, imploding endowments, crumbling buildings, and all around us a secular society self-reporting as spiritual but not religious."[6]

Barna then adds a number of reflections from his studies:

The church landscape will continue to evolve into something that would have been unrecognizable just 25 years ago.

We will see the emergence of new denominations and multi-site churches.

The rise of Hispanic churches may result in a few breakaway denominations that cater to the growing Hispanic population.

There will be continued growth among the charismatic and Pentecostal sector of the Protestant marketplace.

We will continue to see a multiplicity of alternative church forms, led by house churches, marketplace ministries, and cyber-church fellowships.

The end result is a very different universe, in which mainline churches that were solid in recent memory **will lose altitude unless they substantially reinvent themselves.** *(Emphasis mine)*

But he concludes on a positive note:

"Ultimately, some of the pain we have experienced in recent years will produce the joys of the future. The changes that so many lament today will give rise to a more nimble, alert, and adventurous church. There are certainly challenges ahead: especially staying abreast of cultural changes so the church is taken seriously and serves meaningfully."

I love Barna's language, a church that is taken seriously and serves meaningfully. That says it all for me. Can your search committee legitimately claim this is what your congregation is now, or desires to be?

My own concluding recommendations

The first is to beg clergy and lay leaders not to claim "we are different, and none of this applies to us." That's like saying the thermometer reads twenty degrees below zero but it's probably not cold outside. Barna's observations apply to churches across all denominational boundaries.

My second comment is that if your congregation wishes to change, consider taking the example of one congregation I worked with. At the annual meeting, a handout was distributed that listed a number of proposed new initiatives. Under each new idea was a space where congregants could express their interest by noting the amount of much money they would give, and how many hours they would commit to the cause.

This is a form of change with intention that people can buy into. Such an approach also creates an environment of people who will lead, and those who will pitch in as team members.

Finally, I urge clergy and lay leaders to create a culture of encouraging new ideas in your congregation, especially from younger members. This is a "permission granting" culture rather than an attitude that everyone needs close supervision, and that new ideas must pass through multiple layers of approval. Let me provide an example.

I once worked with a church in upstate New York, and a woman told a story about driving her child to school on a cold winter morning. They passed a group of people standing on a street corner without coats, hats, or gloves. The child asked why those people were standing out in the cold. The mother replied that she didn't know, but would find out.

Arriving home, she phoned around and discovered that the people in question were day laborers, hoping for one-day jobs. She got in touch with the agency that oversaw the program, and learned there were sizable numbers of people who lived like this, day to day. She was deeply moved at their plight.

She went to her minister because she knew the church had a New Ministries Seed Fund (All churches should have one!) from which money could be dispersed immediately with the approval of the minister and the board chair. She got a check for $500, added a check for $250 of her own, and called about a dozen people from the church and asked them to support this initiative. Within a day, she had raised $2,500 and gave the money to the agency for cold-weather clothing. This began a new outreach ministry for that particular congregation.

Here was a woman who saw something in the world that was just not right, and was moved to act. God bless her.

I also encourage congregations to consider new initiatives on a trial basis, perhaps six months or so. Church members who are uncertain about new ideas are more willing to give it a try if they believe they can return to previous ways.

One final, excellent idea

One especially effective idea I urge your congregation to consider is giving away the plate offering each Sunday to mission and outreach, excluding checks for pledge payments. This is a powerful ministry, and a lightning-bolt experience for churches that are settled onto a comfortable plateau. Churches implementing this practice have seen plate offerings increase three or four-fold.

If children are present when the offering plate is passed, watching that plate overflow with cash is a magical experience for them. Also, their seeing bighearted adults will help children become generous, and not miserly souls.

Plus, churches that give away the offering usually experience an increase in the annual pledge drive. You will not rob Peter to pay Paul. By giving away the offering each week, your congregants will be successful in its outreach efforts every time they gather in community. They will take immense pride in this.

One last note on giving away the Sunday offering. This is a leadership decision, and the right thing to do. As previously mentioned, if the issue comes to a congregational vote, it will be voted down. This would be a sad day in your church's history.

In conclusion, St. John of the Cross wrote that people who seek God will follow a familiar path, but that path will eventually end and there will be no path. This is my hope, dream, and prayer for your congregation, that you intentionally seek unexplored vistas. Surely, God doesn't want us to be people of diminutive faith and remain on that familiar path for all time.

CHAPTER 5

Not All Denominations
Go About It the Same Way

"Many ministers are on the lookout for a taller steeple church."
— A denominational official who works in ministerial settlement

In this chapter, we'll take a look at how churches in various denominations conduct ministerial searches. Some interesting twists and turns are in store, and search committees can "cut and paste" ideas from one denomination for use in another.

However, your church has its unique nature and character and may not readily fit into an established formula. Search committees also need to determine if they will challenge the established congregational culture in any significant ways.

Let's begin with the first model of searching for a minister, defined as "congregational." After the search committee selects a candidate, the decision to call that minister rests with church members, who vote yea or nay. This method is employed by denominations based on congregational polity, which includes the inherent right of ministers and church members to choose one another freely.

Using this model, at the very beginning of the process, congregants are given survey forms to complete, and church members attend various gatherings to share their thoughts on the type of minister they desire. (As I'll note throughout the book, most congregational surveys fall short of telling a complete story, and congregants sometimes don't want the type of minister they claim they want.) When the search committee has selected a ministerial candidate, usually twelve to twenty-four months later, the congregation is informed as to whom that minister is, and a vote is taken.

Search committees take on an arduous task. In seeking a new pastor, a search committee may review 100 or more ministerial profiles, read and/or listen to countless sermons, call multiple references, and assess each candidate in terms of appropriateness for their particular church.

One committee chairman said he scheduled 150 meetings over a two-year period, and search committee members exchanged 5,000 e-mails. Being a member of a ministerial search committee is not a role to be taken lightly. Stories of search committee "widows" and "widowers" are plentiful. Yet few believe there are shortcuts to the process.

Whatever the period of time involved, the goal of a search committee is to shorten a long list of candidates into a considerably shorter one. Many judgment calls are made along the way. Church people being who they are, search committee members often feel guilty when they eliminate one candidate or another, especially in the later stages of winnowing the list.

Search committees often narrow the field to three candidates. We'll look at various ways they first meet face-to-face in a moment. For now, the ministerial candidate eventually selected and his or her family, if there is one, spend a few days to a week at the church, meeting congregants and determining if this congregation would be a positive settlement. The minister also preaches on one or two Sunday mornings.

Once the candidate's time on-site is completed, a special meeting is called and a vote taken, usually by secret ballot. A favorable vote of 90 percent or more is required for the congregation and the candidate to believe a match has truly been made.

The vote is usually positive, but not always

Most church members trust their search committees, respect the search process, and place a high value on the inordinate amount of work required to find a suitable candidate. However, there are always exceptions.

If the vote comes in at 85 percent or less, meaning that about one church member in five disapproves of the candidate, the congregation and the candidate make the excruciatingly difficult decision that a match has not been made. The minister is not called and the process begins anew.

Thankfully, this does not occur frequently, but when it does, the effect can be devastating in the life of both the minister and the congregation. A great deal of anger and resentment on both sides is often the result.

I'm not going to dwell on a failed call, but it's necessary to take a few moments to note that this potential hazard exists. Search committees may feel they were betrayed by a segment of the congregation that didn't give them a head's up before the vote. This is because a failed vote is rarely the result of random members individually deciding to vote no. It's most likely a concerted effort.

The most reprehensible state of affairs involves a bloc of members who decide they don't like the candidate, garner support in secrecy during the week, and turn out *en masse* to vote against the candidate at the congregational meeting. In general, these blocs tend to be longer-term, relatively inactive members who hearken back to a previous era: as in, "I would never consider a – fill in the blank – woman, black, Asian, single, or gay minister."

Sometimes those voting against the candidate include theological hardliners, who tolerate no deviation from their views. Admittedly, some of these congregants may be following the official denominational stance to the letter. But I question whether they help a congregation envision a new tomorrow, especially if they are a small minority.

With voting members in mind, church leaders should cull the membership roles at the outset of the search process and delete inactive, non-pledging members. Many churches now employ a two-year rule. If members have been absent from church for two years and haven't made a financial contribution, they are dropped from membership. They are not sent a letter asking if they wish to continue their membership under noncommittal terms.

Congregations that permit a "friends" category need to determine if these people are eligible to vote. If friends do not attend church regularly and/or do not make a financial commitment, they also should be ineligible.

In addition, church leaders need to determine how long a person should be a member to be qualified to vote. Denomination standards vary, and church bylaws vary. Check these carefully. My best advice is to be wary of people who want to join the church in the late stages of the search, or after the ministerial candidate has been announced. I do not believe that adding voting members at the eleventh hour should be permitted under any circumstances.

Additional consequences

Let's conclude this section by returning to the minister who was not called by the congregation, along with his or her family. They have put a great deal of time, effort, and emotional energy into believing they would be moving to a new church and community. The fallout can jeopardize a minister's career and cause emotional distress for both the minister and the church.

The congregation is faced with the choice of asking search committee members to give it another try, or constitute a new search committee. In the meantime, an interim minister is likely to remain another year. I recommend that someone from outside the congregation who holds a neutral position assist the congregation in some form of healing process.

Parishioners are unlikely to accomplish reconciliation on their own, especially if passions run high and if members have left the church in anger. I recall one church that formed an online discussion group so members could share their feelings. About three months later, this online format was cancelled, due to the large number of caustic comments and people being "flamed." Anger and resentment should not be allowed to simmer, lying in wait for the next ministerial candidate. Nor should lingering bitterness become an ongoing feature of the culture of any congregation.

A surprising outcome

On occasion, a ministerial candidate may decide that a church that looked so alluring from far away is not that appealing close up, and decline the call. I'm familiar with one church in which the top three choices, in sequence, all declined. This church had an attitude of "won't some minister be fortunate to join our exalted ranks?" Being turned down three times propelled the church into a serious bout of soul-searching, including a revised compensation package.

Denominations that employ the congregational approach include the United Church of Christ (the Congregationalists), the Evangelical Lutheran Church, the Presbyterian Church (USA), the American Baptist Church, and the Disciples of Christ. In each of these faith traditions, the judicatory or synod plays a significant and required role in the process of selecting a minister.

A variation on the congregational approach

The second model is also one that utilizes a congregational survey, as noted above. However, once the survey is completed, church members may or may not remain in the loop. Some congregations arrange for a time in which the candidate can "meet and greet" church members, while others do not. In either instance, church members do not vote final approval.

Similar to the congregational model, the search committee interviews applicants and selects a candidate. The church's governing body then approves the candidate, and a bishop or other high-ranking denominational official extends the call. The Episcopal Church employs this particular approach.

But variations always exist. I'm familiar with one Episcopal church in which, late in the game, the governing body wanted not just one candidate's name, but three names put forward without ranking. I would not recommend this practice, as it places the governing body in the position of replicating the search committee's work. But it bears repeating that many differing approaches may come into play, not all of which can be anticipated, and not all of which may be good decisions.

Getting acquainted

How candidates meet the search committee for the first time involves some interesting contrasts. In some denominations, two members of the search committee, traveling incognito (they hope), visit a candidate's home church. One denomination's guidelines advise, "When you arrive at the Sunday service, try to be unobtrusive, but you will probably be noticed anyway." Committee members attend Sunday service, hear the minister preach, and meet with him or her (or sometimes a co-minister clergy couple) during their time on-site.

One drawback of this approach is the committee as a whole does not meet all potential candidates, and relies on the judgment of the two members who do. When the eventual candidate is selected, he or she travels to the potential new church, meets the full search committee and sees the church and the community for the first time, assuming the minister is not local.

Numerous ministers told me that on their church visit, they led a worship service for a search committee of seven or eight people. One of these services was conducted in a cavernous sanctuary that could seat

1,500 souls. To a person, these ministers found the experience disconcerting. Preaching to a congregation is not an issue. Preaching to ten people or fewer is another experience altogether.

Who travels?

As just noted, in some denominations, search committee members travel to the candidate's home church. In other denominations, it's just the opposite. The search committee stays home, and each ministerial candidate, on separate occasions, travels to the site of the church that is in search.

These visits provide ministers the opportunity to see the church and the community first hand, and meet all the members of the search committee at the same time. Candidates do NOT meet with members of the congregation.

During these visits, each candidate preaches at a "neutral pulpit," a church of the same faith in the region. Search committee members, once again supposedly incognito, attend this service. Acute observers may know full well why a minister from Pennsylvania is preaching in California, or why there are a number of first-time visitors that particular Sunday.

This is a potential breach in the confidentiality of the search process, especially if parishioners at the neutral site know the candidate. If this occurs, discretion is advised, as the minister's home congregation is unlikely to know their minister may soon be leaving them.

The reasoning behind candidates not preaching to the congregation in search is that some ministers may be excellent preachers, but not possess the wider range of skills a congregation requires. In addition, a search committee reviews a candidate's qualifications over weeks and months of time. It is not realistic for a congregation to assess a candidate's suitability in a 20-minute sermon.

Each travel method has merit. Most likely, each is in place due to habit or tradition, not strict denominational policy. Search committees may be able to make a judgment call as to which approach they favor based on whether they wish to travel, or if they prefer candidates to be on the road.

Saying good bye

One interesting difference among congregations is how long the minister who is moving remains with his or her current church. In many congregational churches the search process is seasonal, and the minister receives a call to a new church in the spring. He or she remains until mid-June, often viewed as the traditional end of the church year. The minister moves during the summer and the congregation has ample time to find an interim placement. The interim minister begins work in August or September, the psychological beginning of a new church year.

In other denominations, a minister may announce his or her departure in October, and be gone by December, six weeks later. The general thinking is that a month or so is sufficient for the minister to tie up loose ends and say good-bye. Later on, we'll discuss a primary responsibility of the departing pastor – not to leave behind a difficult situation.

Two additional approaches

A third model might be called "appointive." Ministers in the United Methodist Church and priests in the Roman Catholic Church go where the Bishop tells them to, because they have taken vows of obedience. This approach is based on a bishop's knowledge of ministers in the diocese and a church's particular needs.

For example, a church at one point in its history might benefit from a minister who could assist in growing the congregation numerically. Some years later, that same congregation would benefit from a minister who is more skilled in finance, administration, and conducting a capital campaign.

The appointive approach can create "annual anxiety" in ministerial careers, though some ministers and priests serve the same churches for many years on end. Ministerial distress can arise when ministers with families are asked to move, especially if older children are in high school. The appointive model is not addressed in great detail in this book.

We can also include a fourth model, most frequently used in large churches that do not bear a denominational label. This approach, also not addressed in this book, is the practice of the senior pastor and the congregation grooming successors for key ministerial roles, sometimes over a period of many years. These congregations would never enter into search and bring in an outsider.

Of course, no method guarantees a successful match, and many hybrids exist. I'm familiar with more than one "appointive" church that sought out ministers in other congregations and approached them directly. Conversely, a "congregational" church called a promising, newly graduated seminarian with little input from church members.

One dramatic change in the search process over the years is how candidates and congregations communicate with one another. In decades past, ministers and churches exchanged voluminous amounts of paper, usually heavy three-ring binders. Ministers sent sermons on cassette tapes in the mail. The Internet has changed all that, with electronic exchanges and Skype interviews becoming the norm. Search committee members can now read sermons or watch videos of ministers preaching on church websites at their convenience.

An interesting twist

In some denominations, candidates send their ministerial profiles directly to any church of any size in any geographic area of the country. In other denominations, regional judicatory officials serve as gatekeepers, allowing only certain names to be presented to one church or another. Inconsistency prevails, even within denominations.

For example, a judicatory in one faith tradition screen candidates, while a neighboring judicatory of that same faith tradition does not. In some traditions, judicatory officials forward all ministerial profiles, but each official has a great deal of discretion and may forward some profiles before others. Complaints of favoritism are common. This is not a job I would want to have.

In some faith traditions, judicatory officials have been told by congregations not to forward the profiles of gay or lesbian ministers. In other faith traditions, this request is disregarded, and judicatory officials forward all profiles to congregations in search. The reasoning, in part, is because not all gay clergy have self-identified. Plus, in some denominations, sexual preference is not viewed as a barrier to effective ministry. (See Chapter 12 for a fuller discussion of this issue.)

Some denominations also permit ministers of other faiths to apply. The Episcopalians and the Lutherans are in full communion. The United Church of Christ (Congregational) is in communion with the Evangelical Lutheran Church, the Presbyterian Church (USA), and the Disciples of Christ.

Whichever approach is utilized, search committee members and ministers in search may feel like they are venturing into unfamiliar territory. The best-laid plans rarely proceed as expected, detours are ever present, and sometimes people drive on the wrong side of the road. I recall one candidate who was picked up at the airport by an elderly member of the congregation who could have won the Most Terrifying Driver Award. By the time this candidate arrived at the church for an interview, he was a nervous wreck and made a poor appearance.

If all of this sounds tedious and inordinately time-consuming, you might consider joining the Church of Jesus Christ of Latter Day Saints (Mormons), or any number of other faith traditions that have no ordained clergy and never enter into the search process at all.

CHAPTER 6

The Stakes are High

*"There is no more critical moment in the life of a congregation
than the moment in which it faces going from one pastor to another."*
–Loren Mead

M ead's point of view is echoed frequently in church literature. Many churchgoers recall eras in congregational life by noting the pastor at the time. They remember that Rev. Foster focused on Bible study, and that Pastor Allison started the Vacation Bible School. Father Johnson got us involved in social programs, and Pastor Benedict emphasized Sunday school for children and youth. The Smiths were killed in an auto accident when Pastor Hutchins was here.[1]

It's not just ministers who come and go that mark the eras. It's also how those ministers said good-bye that is etched in the memories of churchgoers. People in the pews remember Pastor Smith's retirement party with great fondness: the thoughtfully prepared homemade refreshments, the memory book of photographs she was given, and all the good wishes that came forth.

Parishioners would rather forget the time when Pastor Dalton was on the scene one day and gone the next, and the accusations, hard feelings, and guilt that accompanied his family leaving town. It took many years for the church to recover from that one. To paraphrase Tolstoy, all happy ministers leave in the same happy way, while all unhappy ministers leave in their unique, unhappy way.

Author Joseph Umidi writes, "The first step in a successful leadership transition is an effective strategy for dealing with the past."[2] Some churches have a relatively calm past, while others lurch from one predicament to the next. How your congregation deals with the past will be a major factor in the caliber of minister you are able to call.

The importance of how churches deal with the past, especially an unhappy past, is the subject of numerous books and cannot be overstated. In this book, we'll touch on the past in smaller increments as we go along. For now, suffice it to say that congregations are human institutions. They have their strengths and weaknesses, their quirks, their failings, and their hopes and dreams for tomorrow.

So let's continue with the subject at hand; the future of your church. A significant part of this future is the minister who will be called, and the high stakes for all involved in the search process.

I. THE RISKS FOR THE SEARCH COMMITTEE

There is no lay role with such long-range potential for ensuring the future of the congregation than being on the search committee.[3] A change of pastors is an exciting time in the life of a congregation, with much anticipation. The search committee feels this too. But in the back of their minds, their greatest fear is making a bad choice – choosing a minister who will be unsuccessful and leave after a short ministry, possibly under difficult circumstances.

If this occurs, search committee members may feel they have let the congregation down. They believe their fellow congregants will be upset with them for not performing due diligence and making a poor choice.

Making a bad choice based on the traditional method of the congregational survey and parishioners' comments is one thing. If the stakes are already high under these conditions, they are stratospheric by calling a minister who is out of the congregation's frame of reference entirely.

Are you beginning to think it would be a good idea to include the possibility of calling a revolutionary minister on the survey form, and in conversations with church members? I sincerely hope so.

> *If you do not include the congregation in the discussion about whether to call a minister with revolutionary ideas, church members will be deprived of exploring the true range of ministry for your church.*

Here's why. I'm a fan of Paul Nixon, an "out there" minister who changed the worship format from Sunday to Sunday, so when people showed up, it was a surprise what was going to happen. The congregation loved it.[4]

I also recall a 69-year old woman who had gone to a Bruce Springsteen concert on Saturday night, and the next morning in church said, "Why can't we have music like that around here sometimes?" Your congregation may be more adventurous than meets the eye.

One of the worst mistakes a search committee can make is to adopt the attitude, "Our congregation is not ready for…"

I don't wish to dwell on bad choices, but looking into the disheartening subject of why searches fail is an excellent vehicle to illustrate a wide array of issues that search committees will face. It's also a head's up to avoid some obvious pitfalls.

Why searches fail: let us count the ways

The first reason search committees veer off track, as we've touched on, is because they take at face value the results of the congregational survey, along with parishioners' opinions regarding the type of minister they desire. I've seen dozens of surveys over the years, from churches of many denominations. Most are surprisingly similar. Congregants desire exceptional preaching, a pastoral presence, kindness, and warmth in the minister. The search committee, in turn, seeks these traits in ministerial candidates.

Congregational size is a determining factor

Let's take a momentary but important bypass in this discussion to note that search committee members are too often unaware that the size of their congregation determines in large part the ministerial personality that will be the most successful. In general, smaller congregations do well with the minister described above, pastoral and warm. These are ministers who remember your cousin's name when she visits once a year.

However, as a church reaches a Sunday worship attendance of 150 or more, it becomes a "Program" church; and at 300 or more, a "Corporate" church, sometimes called a resource congregation, and requires a minister with proven leadership and managerial skills. A defining characteristic of ministers in large churches is their rightfully assuming significant authority in all aspects of congregational life.[5]

Many rank and file members believe that as a church grows numerically, the minister's role will remain more or less the same. They expect the minister will continue to be a pastoral presence in the lives of parishioners. But in large congregations, even the most capable minister cannot possibly know hundreds of members personally, let alone provide them pastoral care on a continuing basis.

Large churches require skilled leaders who can maintain current initiatives, begin new ministries, manage a more complex organization, raise more money, supervise staff, and possibly redefine the purpose of the congregation entirely. Pastoral care takes on a lesser role, and members may be unhappy that the minister is not available on a walk-in basis.

I recall speaking with a search committee about this very issue, in a church that had grown numerically. A committee member who preferred the smaller congregation of yesterday (Why was he on the search committee?) said, "Can't we have a minister who's always there for us and run the church, too?" He seemed skeptical when I told him the church was unlikely to find all these qualities in one candidate.

Issues of size raise an interesting conundrum for search committees. Can a minister who has served a smaller church meet the demands of a larger congregation? A number of search committee members told me that smaller churches don't always present leadership challenges, and that ministers have not developed the skills necessary for a larger-church ministry.

However, ministers in small congregations often seek greater challenges because they find the small church too settled into established ways. Thus, a compelling question that search committees in larger congregations might face is whether they will pass by an engaging, smaller-church minister who shows potential. Or might that search committee take a risk, hoping the minister will develop leadership skills on the job?

With congregational size in mind, I've only met one minister who willingly moved from a larger church to a smaller one. He told his growing congregation that he was a pastoral minister at heart, and felt out of his element as the congregation grew larger and more multifaceted.

Back to the subject at hand

The second reason search committees go adrift is similar to the first: the deluge of congregants' views and opinions they receive. This time, it's not just the type of minister that members desire. It's the vision of the church's future.

Search committee members will receive a plethora of conflicting views. As noted, these include the written congregational survey, along with opinions expressed in small groups at the beginning of the process. Committee members will also be on the receiving end of verbal comments from mostly well-meaning parishioners at coffee hour following Sunday services for months on end.

Usually, parishioners' comments refer to the church doing more of something or less of something in which the church is already engaged. Sometimes, parishioners bring good ideas from other churches. People might also put forward the names of ministers in other churches they believe would be suitable candidates. In all probability, these comments will include some very good ideas, some off-the-wall suggestions, and maybe a gripe or two.

Some parishioners believe that a change of pastor might be an excellent time to address pet peeves they've carried around for a good long while. Maybe the new minister will take down that ghastly painting in the vestibule that a congregant's nephew donated a few years ago. Or maybe the new minister will inform the choir, whose members practice on Sunday morning before the service, to stop filling up the parking lot and making the rest of us walk so far. Readers, no doubt, can add many other peeves to this list.

Added to this ever-flowing fountain of advice is that many parishioners believe their vision of the future is *absolutely correct, even if they are completely wrong*. They expect search committees to heed their views. Congregants' views can loom large in search committee deliberations, especially the views of opinionated members.

The most shameful example

The third reason searches fail is that search committees gloss over or deliberately hide unpleasant aspects of congregational life in order to attract high-quality candidates. Likewise, some ministers are disingenuous, overestimating their skill and experience, underestimating their deficiencies, or minimizing their failures.

If a poor match is made under these circumstances, each party has done the congregation a grave disservice, and have only themselves to blame. Sadly, the people in the pews will pay the greatest price for their dishonesty.

The stakes are proportional

Let's return to congregational size once again, to further define the type of minister who might be the most successful in a particular setting. We'll also look at the risks involved in the search process from church to church, depending on a congregation's size, nature, and character.

The basics of the search process are sound, but each ministerial search needs to be tailored to a congregation's individual circumstances. I believe the stakes are proportional and play out in different ways. Let's consider a few examples, starting with large "cathedral-like" congregations and concluding with smaller, local churches.

Large churches, highly visible congregations, and cathedral churches

Some churches are considered plum assignments and carry high esteem for ministers fortunate enough to be called. These churches are often landmark structures, with long histories of service to the community and beyond.

These congregations are sometimes called "dominant" churches because they attract a sizable number of the community's civic, cultural, and political leaders. In some parts of the South, these churches are characterized by parishioners' dress on Sunday morning – suits and ties for men, dresses and sometimes hats for women. Robed choirs and classical music are integral to the worship experience. This is high church.

As mentioned earlier, this book does not address large independent or non-denominational churches because they groom ministerial leadership from within. They do not enter into search and would never bring in an outsider. Some of these churches serve as denominations unto themselves, providing ministerial training instead of sending aspiring ministers to a traditional seminary. Some of these churches are mega-churches, have thousands of members, immense buildings, and are a significant presence in their communities.

Beyond the prestige of being called to a dominant church, ministers may derive offers to write books, lead events at seminaries, play visible roles at various gatherings, and be considered for high office in the denomination. Ministers who are called have achieved the pinnacle of their profession, for all to witness.

Cathedral churches offer attractive compensation packages and usually call seasoned ministers with exemplary track records. The expectations include exceptional preaching skills and being a moral and scholarly voice in the community.

For this reason, paradoxically, the chances of a search committee making a poor choice are less than in smaller churches. This is because the pool contains only top-tier candidates, most of whom currently serve a church of equal size. Surprisingly, many large churches are quite amenable to significant change, and expect the minister to function as a strong leader who envisions a new tomorrow. This new tomorrow often comes in the form of a major capital campaign or significantly expanded, big-ticket mission efforts in foreign countries.

It's unlikely that a minister of this caliber will prove to be incompetent, and only a foolhardy pastor would become involved in financial, sexual, or highly controversial misconduct because these ministers make headlines coming and going. It is very difficult to keep a secret in a cathedral church, and egregious conduct may signal the end of a ministerial career.

Even if a minister "didn't work out" and it happens, cathedral-like churches are highly resilient. They benefit from a significant heritage, and usually have the financial resources, professional expertise, and where-withal to weather even hurricane-force gales.

Also, with a large membership, most people in the pews do not have a close relationship with the minister. Church members may be distressed if the minister departs, but it doesn't feel as though they are losing a close personal friend. A newly constituted search committee is likely to enjoy reviewing another roster of the highest quality candidates available.

The suburban church

A failed ministry is just the opposite in small to mid-sized churches, a large number of which are located in suburban and rural areas. Ministry in these congregations is highly personal. Ministers form deep friendships with parishioners and their families, having conducted weddings, baptisms, and funerals over many years. Ministers tend to leave small and pastoral-sized congregations for three main reasons. Let's begin with the most emotionally charged.

Passions run high

Small to mid-sized congregations demonstrate most clearly why the clergy role is markedly different from a secular job. Few in the secular world are called to the hospital late at night to console a couple whose newborn child has died. (I know a minister who has done this three times.) Few in the secular world are first in line to be called in times of tragedy, grief, and devastating loss.

In the secular world, it's also unlikely that employees or customers will seek your counsel in regard to marital problems, alcoholism, domestic abuse, or a variety of dysfunctional family issues that ministers frequently encounter.

One minister described his experience compellingly as, "The most surprising thing about ministry is the deep hurt that people walk around with. People who appear quite well adjusted have shared courageous stories of pain – wounds that don't' seem to go away, no matter how good and pious and prayerful they are. Many in the church have been to hell and back, and they go on in silence, suffering alone."[6]

Parishioners' needs arise at all times of the day and night, at any time of the year. I recall a church in which the female minister got married, and a parishioner came through the receiving line following the ceremony. The parishioner said to the bride, "Oh, Jennifer, I'm so happy for you, and, and…my mother is dying!" At this, the parishioner burst into tears. She may have expected the minister to step out of the receiving line and console her.

The highly charged emotional context of parish ministry far exceeds that of most secular roles, except for counselors and therapists, and is where great risks lie.

As an example, I recall the story of a woman whose husband died tragically, leaving her with four young children. The minister, new to the church, didn't know the woman or her family, and pastoral care was not his strong suit. He was at a loss for words and on a few occasions evidently said, "I just don't know what to say."

The grieving widow reported this to numerous members in the church, and added, "There were a lot of things he could have said." The minister gained the reputation of being distant, which put his ministry under a cloud. He never fully gained the trust of the congregation, and left two years later.

This is an example of a simple human failing with only one church member that carried long-term, irreparable consequences for an entire congregation.

Small to mid-sized congregations can be extremely vulnerable. Parishioners place great trust in ministers, and hold them to a high standard of conduct. Church members can forgive many personal shortcomings in the minister, even divorce, but may feel personally betrayed if a minister fails in his or her professional role.

If a clergy failure is particularly egregious, with sexual misconduct perceived as the worst, a congregation may split into various factions, some supporting the minister while others demanding his or her ouster. Church members might angrily leave the congregation, never to return.

As we've discussed, a minister leaving under difficult circumstances becomes a chapter in that congregation's past. Congregations urgently need to resolve feelings of anger, resentment, grief, and distrust. One minister leaving unhappily may lead to a sequence of subsequent ministers leaving unhappily. A dysfunctional culture, once established, is astonishingly efficient at reproducing itself.[7] Sadly, I've worked with churches in which some issues of the past may never be resolved.

If clergy misconduct becomes known in the community, a number of added high-stake issues also come into play for the small to medium-sized church. First is the inability to attract new members. Who wants to join a church in conflict? Second, there's likely to be a decrease in the number of ministerial candidates who will consider serving a troubled congregation. Search committees may find the range of candidates to be less experienced, less capable, and have checkered histories of their own.

The minister just didn't understand us

The next reason ministers leave include close cousins to the above comment, such as "he never got to know us," or "she never felt comfortable around us." Also in this category might be differences in worship or preaching styles, theological views, leadership issues, church vision, and sometimes just the need for a change.

It's not always the congregation that decides a minister should leave. Sometimes, ministers realize they will not fulfill their call to ministry in a particular church. And sometimes, congregations are not adventuresome enough for a gifted pastor who wishes to envision a new tomorrow. I recall one pastor saying to his congregation, "I use only a fraction of my ministerial skills here, and feel underutilized. I need to be in a church where I can be a more complete minister." Some ministers struggle financially, and seek other settlements primarily for larger compensation packages.

We might also add the category of ministers who stay too long. Sometimes, ministers have accomplished all they ever will with a congregation, but remain nevertheless. This is often because of inertia, fear of finding another church, a desire for children to finish school, a weakened call to ministry, or not wishing to move to a different geographic area.

A minister who stays too long presents the church with a significant dilemma. Usually, the issue is to continue with a diminished ministry vs. the guilt a congregation may feel in forcing the minister to leave.

Such leave-takings may or may not be agreeable, but they are usually less volatile than an outright dismissal or issues of misconduct. Sometimes, ministers believe they haven't been given an adequate chance, and they may be right. I've known congregations that became embittered, rather than forgiving, toward a minister over issues that I didn't believe were all that substantive. But in most instances, the minister and lay leaders have attempted good-faith efforts to resolve their differences.

If the congregation has asked the minister to resign for reasons other than misconduct, a visible gesture of that congregation doing the right thing is to provide the outgoing minister a generous severance package, along with an offer to give favorable references. Having done so, the search committee that is eventually formed is likely to enjoy a list of strong ministerial candidates. This is an excellent way to deal with the past. Likewise, departing ministers should speak highly of their former congregations.

The minister has been successful

In small and pastoral settings, with ministry based on close relationships, even pastors moving to new congregations after a successful ministry may be viewed as turning their backs on church members. This is especially the case if the announcement is a surprise to church members, which it usually is. Adding to the unhappiness are denominational guidelines that prohibit a minister from making contact with a previous congregation for a certain period of time.

I've heard pastors say that during the third and fourth years of their ministries, they experienced an increase in the number of counseling appointments made by parishioners. It takes awhile for a minister to gain the trust of a congregation. Once established, if the pastor moves on, parishioners may feel that trust has been irreparably broken. How long will it be before church members trust another minister? This is especially the case in congregations with a history of high turnover.

Some ministers claim the stakes are the highest in moving to a congregation where a beloved minister preceded them. In most instances, a two-year interim ministry is sufficient to resolve members' longing for a previous pastor. If a minister is called directly following a highly regarded pastorate, often because the search committee claims we're a healthy church and everything's fine, that minister is likely to become the short-term, interim pastor. It can take a long time for a congregation to say goodbye, especially if they believe they are saying goodbye to a golden age.

Divine discontent

Regardless of whether a minister leaves or stays, a powerful way to create a new future is based on a sizeable number of congregants experiencing some form of displeasure. As in, "I'm mad as hell and can't take it anymore." Emerson once said, "Most people wish to be settled. Only as people are unsettled is there any hope for them." This should be excellent news to any search committee getting ready to gear up.

Church people get restless for many reasons. They may visit a nearby church and discover something they wish their church did. They might learn of a smaller congregation that has a larger mission program. They wonder why their youth group has ten kids, while the youth group in a comparable church down the road has fifty. Once churchgoers latch onto a powerful idea, they can pursue it with great vigor.

This restlessness may come from the congregation, and also from the minister. I recall a story of a minister who was successful by all measures. But he was agonizingly discontent for reasons he couldn't fathom, and thought about leaving the ministry altogether. A friend of his worked for an advertising agency, and thought the minister would be great in this line of work. At the first meeting the minister attended as a guest, the subject of discussion was how a major brewer could sell more beer to Hispanics.

Completely disillusioned, he returned to his congregation, and the following Sunday preached to his congregants about his distress. He said the congregation could take great pride in all they had accomplished together. But he also said he wanted to be a different kind of person, to be closer to God, but just didn't know how to do that.

After the service, he received an outpouring of emotion from his congregation, who said they felt similar longings. The minister began to serve as a chaplain to the local police and fire departments. He began to visit prisoners in a local jail. His sermons and his spiritual journey served as a beacon for others who wanted to find greater meaning in their lives. The congregation went through a period of discernment, soul-searching, and prayer about what kind of congregation God was calling them to become. Wouldn't you love to be part of a congregation like this?

New and emerging churches

The final category of congregations that seek ministers include newly formed, storefront, inner-city churches that serve a particular segment of the population, or people with significant needs. These churches take risks with young, unproven, or inexperienced ministers because of their adventuresome spirits and fire-in-the-belly attitudes.

Ministers who accept such a call will probably work long hours under difficult circumstances for low compensation because of a powerful sense of what God is calling them to do. Ministers may not be expected to stay all that long. Turnover is often high because these churches are so demanding. Sometimes, their main function is just to survive.

Of course, there are innumerable variations among some 350,000 communities of faith in the United States. The norm is a church of between 25 and 125 people at Sunday worship attendance, regardless of denomination. Each congregation has its particular personality, nature, and the way they go about things.

While not a subject of this book, many para-church ministries also exist, such as college chaplaincies, hospital chaplaincies, ministries at camps and conference centers, and military chaplaincies. Unlike being "called" by a congregation, these jobs are paid staff positions and usually do not involve a lengthy search process as does the parish.

II. HIGH STAKES FOR THE MINISTER

Let's start with the minister's spouse and family coming along as part of the deal. They are expected to play highly visible, supporting roles. This is comparable to a poker player betting the bank on having the winning hand.

Most certainly, non-clergy families frequently move to different geographic areas and take new jobs. But if that job doesn't work out, other employment opportunities may be nearby, for one spouse or the other. They don't necessarily have to move again. And it's not as though either parent brings their kids to work on weekends.

Thankfully, life for clergy families has improved over time. The good old days, when the minister's wife was expected to be a full-time, unpaid, long-suffering volunteer are long gone. But even with an increasing number of ministerial spouses being men, and despite many clergy spouses having their own careers, the clergy family remains an integral component of the parish experience. An absent clergy spouse is a significant liability to the minister, whatever the denomination.

Regardless of the church size or setting, a new minister also becomes instantly recognizable to every member of the congregation, be it 5,000 members, 500 members, or 50 members. This is not to mention the extended family members and friends of congregants, who will get a full report on the new minister when he or she arrives. Secular jobs, unless extremely high level, rarely accord this level of visibility and scrutiny.

Clergy visibility extends beyond the workplace and into the community, as well. The smaller the town, the greater the visibility. Even relative newcomers to town will eventually recognize the local priest, rabbi, and minister, and maybe even PK's – preacher's kids. Clergy families live their lives in goldfish bowls.

Some ministers claim that high visibility is a blessing, but one that also carries occupational hazards. Many ministers and their families are exemplary role models in their communities and enjoy great respect among parishioners and non-parishioners alike.

But ministers also report being questioned pointedly in the grocery store or other public places about issues of religion, ethics, and morals, sometimes by complete strangers. On airplanes, ministers have been known to be disingenuous about their profession to passengers seated nearby. An increasing number of ministers report tedious conversations with the "spiritual but not religious" crowd.

In years gone by, mercifully, church members tended to believe that ministers should be humble servants, and an unspoken attitude was that everyone in the church was the minister's boss. The minister was viewed as an underling. Also long gone is the belief that ministers should seek spiritual and not material rewards, and earn no more than the lowest-paid member of the congregation.

However, some outdated attitudes continue to persist. In secular jobs, employees might not like the boss or their co-workers, but they are careful about who they tell. In church, if parishioners have a grudge against the minister, they feel entitled to tell as many people as they like, as often as they like.

Some church members also believe they have free license to speak to the minister or spouse any way they wish. I recall an incident in which the minister's spouse wore a red dress to a Christmas holiday event. A church member excoriated her, claiming, "The color red is only for harlots!"

A minister who wears a clergy collar is likely to be an immediate conversation stopper. Even clergy who do not wear clerical garb find people guarded in conversation, on their best behavior. This adds to the fact that clergy have many acquaintances but few friends. Such attitudes are completely understandable, as church members wish to keep a professional distance.

A brief conclusion

All this is to say that it's helpful for search committee members and ministers alike to better understand one another's perspectives. Doing so helps remove common barriers that contribute to making the search process too shallow, a frequent complaint from both sides of the table.

CHAPTER 7

We Want to Grow!

"A lot of churches claim they want to grow, but nobody
wants all those strangers around here."
—Church author Edward Hammett

We might begin this brief chapter on church growth by questioning whether your congregation wants to grow numerically or not. Small to medium-sized churches, up to 400 members or so, can be quite comfortable with their current size, thank you very much, and give lip service to growth at best.

Churches of this size tend to function on a maintenance model. Authors Weese and Crabtree describe this state of affairs as:

Continuity over innovation

Security over risk

The past over the future

An attitude of passivity or even hostility toward newcomers[1]

To me, this demonstrates a shocking disregard for people who are lost and lonely, but this is the nature and character of small congregations.

Family-sized churches and pastoral churches often act as closed systems, and can view newcomers with suspicion. I once had a string of eight consecutive church visits in which not a single person spoke to me during the coffee hour, even though I was wearing a visitor's nametag or holding a red coffee mug. My experience is the norm in North American Protestantism. On a few occasions, I called ministers the following day and recounted my experience. The responses were, invariably, "I just can't imagine that happening. We're such a friendly church." Of course they are friendly, among themselves.

Many people, especially adults who are single or divorced, claim they feel the most lonely in church. Such a sad irony. If people are treated rudely or experience loneliness once, they won't return for a repeat performance. Church-shoppers have many choices. You may have only one chance with that visitor.

Even among churches claiming they wish to grow, a common attitude regarding potential new members is "if people are lucky, they'll find us; if not, there's nothing we can do about that, is there?" Such aloofness is a debilitating factor in congregational growth. When I ask clergy and lay leaders who the next 25 members might be, the answer is, invariably "whoever shows up." This is a growth strategy?

A colleague of mine told a story about working with a congregation in which membership had been in decline for ten years. He showed the church's board members a bar graph to this effect, illustrating the downward trend. He then asked each of the nine church leaders to draw an approximation of what that bar graph would look like over the next ten years, if the church did nothing differently. Eight of the nine drew bar graphs that showed the church returning to previously high levels of membership. Hope springs eternal, I suppose.

Many churches believe they are open to new members, including racial minorities, but no one does anything differently and membership stays on a plateau. Later on, church members may exclaim, "But we're so open to new members! Why aren't people showing up?"

A very different view

Churches can grow by reaching out to various cohorts of the population.[2] These cohorts might include:

> *Single-parent families*
> *People recently widowed or divorced*
> *Empty-nester couples*
> *People in interfaith or interracial marriages*
> *Families with a member who has a physical disability*
> *Families with a member who struggles with alcoholism*
> *Cancer survivors*
> *Military families*
> *Men between the ages of 30-40*
> *Recent immigrants*

The list is endless. Because of your church's geographic location, it may have something extremely valuable to offer one cohort or another. You may discover a sizable number of people in a given cohort in your geographic area are not being served by another church. If you currently have people in your congregation who represent any of these cohorts and who are willing to reach out, it will be easier to attract others in that same cohort.

Merely claiming your church is open to everyone is insufficient. Also, the ground rules do not permit you to say, "We have an open and affirming faith, and should attract all these groups and anyone else, for that matter."

Most parishioners are extremely reluctant to invite their friends, neighbors, or colleagues to church. But it is perfectly acceptable to say, "Our church hosts a dinner for single-parent families (or any other cohort) on the first Saturday of each month. The purpose is not to evangelize. Rather, we believe there's a lot of loneliness out there, and we want to help alleviate that." Someone who attends such a dinner might become your church's newest member and perhaps someday its largest financial donor.

Another effective way to engage new people is to invite them to participate in a mission or outreach project. The more generations involved, the better. Many newcomers find this a preferable alternative to attending the Sunday worship service.

Waiting for people to show up? Surely, your church will not remain isolated and removed from those who are seeking the presence of God, will it?

CHAPTER 8

Who Should Be
on the Search Committee?

"Church members often say they want young pastors – except young
pastors bring new ideas, but church members don't want that."
—Duke University Pulpit and Pew Study

I hope the above quote is as exasperating to you as it is to me. I believe this attitude is an inexcusable aspect of congregational life in America today. But this book is for dauntless souls who envision a very different future for their churches. Just be aware that you're standing against the tide – a mighty tide.

I'm a hopeful person in regard to search committees doing well. I've met many dedicated, committed, and earnest souls who wish to do the right thing. But about 95 percent of people who find themselves on search committees have never done it before, and most will never do it again.[1] There's a steep learning curve. Let's review two basic ground rules, then discuss how search committees should be constituted.

Size of the search committee

In small churches with fewer than 150 people at Sunday worship, a committee of five members may be sufficient. For congregations attracting between 150 and 500 at Sunday services, a committee of seven to nine people should be adequate. For large congregations, I've heard of search committees having as many as fifteen members, though this sounds a bit unwieldy to me.

In general, the larger the committee, the easier tasks can be parceled out and the lighter the overall burden. The flip side is that the larger the committee, the more difficult communications become, and the less likelihood that all members can attend meetings.

How much does a search cost?

The largest expenses will be travel costs, whether search committee members are on the road, or if candidates travel to churches that are in search. If the search committee selects three candidates they wish to meet, it's simple math to calculate airfare, lodging, and routine travel expenses.

Some search committee budgets include moving expenses for the minister eventually chosen, and routine costs involved with the clergy family relocating. If you look in any denominational magazine, you'll notice numerous van line ads offering discounts for clergy. When I realized how many ads there were, I wasn't sure if this was good news or bad news.

Other expenses may include long distance phone calls, postage, and office supplies, but these are likely to be modest in nature. I think it's permissible for the search committee to have dinner or plan a social event on occasion, to have an enjoyable time together beyond their demanding roles.

It's also important to realize the hidden costs associated with a congregation in transition. A common belief is that a church will save money on the departing minister's compensation package. This may not be the case, as the cost of an interim minister and temporary housing may be comparable. Churches may also experience a decline in worship attendance of 10-15 percent, with a potential decrease of 10-15 percent in pledging, as congregants take a wait-and-see attitude toward who the new minister will be.[2]

Church leaders might wish to remind parishioners to stay on the team during a period of ministerial transition. Don't you think this should go without saying? Why is the Lord's work so hard sometimes?

If your policy is to bring ministerial candidates to your hometown, I urge you not to offer home hospitality ~~unless living quarters have a separate entrance~~. Interviews and meetings can go on for days at a time, sometimes late into the evening. Candidates need a restful place where they can be "off duty." This is not possible as a guest in a parishioner's home.

I also urge search committees not to economize by housing candidates in substandard lodging. How you welcome candidates speaks volumes about how you value that candidate's presence. Astute candidates will certainly notice if everything is done on the cheap, which indicates a congregation that functions in a similar manner. This could be a factor in a qualified candidate saying no.

How search committee members are selected

There are no hard-and-fast rules from denomination to denomination. The most common practice is a special nominating committee or a group of board members who make recommendations. These recommendations are usually based on a church member's service to the congregation, judgment, character, and the respect of their fellow congregants. The church's full board then approves the nominations. Being selected to serve on the search committee is a notable honor, indeed.

One denomination recommends open elections. Church members are given blank ballots and asked to fill in names. Those who receive the most votes are then asked to serve. With all due respect, this approach strikes me as too indeterminate, and may not assure a search committee with a balanced perspective.

Once the committee is gathered, members often select one from their ranks to serve as chair. But in more that one instance, a board president first asked a respected parishioner to chair the search committee. The newly selected chair and a group of board members then chose the remaining members of the committee. While this approach has merit, the tendency exists for established members to select only church members they already know.

Criteria for membership

Many nominating bodies select search committee members from various program areas of the church. Thus, the committee might consist of representatives from the Sunday school and youth programs, the choir, buildings and grounds, finance, membership, adult education, mission and outreach, and someone who is familiar with computers and information technology. Some churches might add a longer-term member who is retired, a fairly new member of the church, and one or more gay or lesbian members.

Churches should resist the temptation to ask a sizable number of retirees to serve on the search committee mainly because they have the time. A one-generation perspective is not sufficient for a multi-generation church.

Selecting people who represent program areas of the church is a seemingly common sense approach. This ensures that a variety of voices and church concerns are taken into account. However, there are some drawbacks. The Sunday school representative might wish for a younger minister who can relate to children and youth. The finance representative may desire a minister who can raise more money. The membership representative may wish for a minister who will attract new members to the congregation.

Thus, search committee members may be all over the map. This is not a bad thing in itself, but the downside is that some members may lobby for their particular constituency above the interests of the congregation as a whole.

Thus, ministerial candidates should not assume an unbiased perspective on the part of all search committee members. Some might have agendas, which may be difficult to determine.

Before the search committee meets for the first time, each member has likely conjured up a portrait of the minister who would best serve the congregation. One observer noted, "What's your vision of who our new minister should be? That's a profound question. It's also a secret that every member of the search committee holds. The sooner this secret is shared, the better."[3]

At the outset of the committee's work, it is also essential to determine if members are flexible in their views about the minister who should be called. As we've discussed throughout the book, the type of minister being considered should include candidates who bring a perspective the congregation has never before considered.

A very different selection process

Some churches believe that representatives from various program areas will not result in the necessary skills required for search committees to do their work effectively. They prefer a search committee that includes people with experience in Human Resources, or who have expertise in evaluating potential employees.

In addition to the HR perspective, search committees might include people at supervisory levels in their professional jobs who have interviewed and hired employees, and have specialized assessment skills. A third area of expertise might be someone who is knowledgeable about employee benefits, pension, and insurance issues. Yet another area of expertise might be someone who has some type of experience with clergy families, and understands their unique circumstances.

Once again, there are no cast-in-stone rules regarding the make-up of the search committee. However, potential members should not be considered merely on the basis of the church program they represent. Beyond professional skills, members of search committees told me they appreciated their fellow members' even temperaments, their willingness to take on tasks, their being slow to anger and quick to forgive, their readiness to support one another, their attention to detail, their ability to handle large amounts of information, their skill at maintaining confidentiality, and their ability to pray together.

Who should not be on the search committee

Let's begin with people who either loved or hated the previous minister. These souls should not be asked to participate because the inclination would be to call someone "just like Pastor Jones, who served us so well." Or, just the opposite, "anyone but a person like Pastor Smith, who left us high and dry." Both views become blinders to a wider range of ministerial possibilities.

Poor candidates include those with rigid, inflexible, or extremely forceful personalities; and those who know in their heart of hearts exactly the minister who would be just right, before the search even begins. Do not allow anyone to join the committee who begs, borrows, steals, cajoles, threatens, or self-identifies themselves to persuade church leaders for a coveted committee spot.

There's also the category of people who served on previous search committees. Are they good choices or not? The answer to that question, in part, depends on how long ago the previous search was held. If it was ten years or more, chances are that search committee member's perspective may reflect a previous era. All things considered, I'd opt for an entirely new search committee, including some newer members.

The search committee will need to make a unanimous or near-unanimous decision regarding who the next minister will be. Search committees can take some educated advice from Baptist ministers Riley Walker and Marcia Patton in this regard. They write, "Often the church will vote the same way a committee is divided. If the call is from a committee of five members, only four of whom agree on the candidate, the congregational vote is likely to be 80 percent, which means that 20 percent of members will have strong doubts about the minister before he or she even begins."[4]

Beware of the extremely influential church member(s)

I once worked with a church for over two years, and came to know many members quite well. This church went into search toward the end of my time with them. Upon seeing who was appointed to the search committee, I knew they would make a poor choice in the ministerial candidate. And they did.

All the members of this search committee were in their fifties and sixties, except for a token thirty-something, and they fondly recalled a bygone era when the congregation was smaller and more intimate. They revered a former minister who was kindly, pastoral, and who asked little of them. This committee nominated a minister of their own generation from a small congregation who shared many of their memories. He was a very sweet guy. He lasted just over two years.

The search committee failed in two significant ways. It downplayed the congregation's complexity, and it skimmed over a number of extremely problematic issues. From day one, the minister was in over his head.

This minister did not help his cause, in an affluent community and with an attractive compensation package, by wearing frayed, rumpled, ill-fitting clothes. Some parishioners believed he reflected poorly on the congregation. I'm also familiar with a church that called a minister from a distant state. Two years later, the minister still displayed out-of-state license plates on her car. She had only a short-term ministry.

An unfortunate outcome of this extremely nice-guy minister was the way in which he was let go. An influential member of the congregation didn't like him, and recommended that a congregational survey be taken. The supposedly innocuous reason was "just to see how people feel about things in the church." In my experience, no matter how phrased, congregational surveys are almost always a referendum on the minister.

People who wish to get rid of a minister bring considerable stamina to the task. This influential member conducted his own behind-the-scenes survey, including scores of phone calls, without the minister's knowledge. He compiled a sizable number of complaints, many of which were questionable, and presented them to the board chair. Within a short time, the minister was asked to resign. And guess who turned up as the chair of the next search committee?

As Loren Mead reminds us, churches can be commandeered by a surprisingly small number of people.[5] Sometimes, these people can be members of the same family, especially in smaller congregations.

Ministers underestimate the influence of powerful personalities at their peril. Surveys reveal that as many as 43 percent of ministers who were terminated were forced out by conflict with a small but influential faction of the congregation. In some instances, only one or two board members have forced ministers to leave.[6] I urge ministers and search committees to include language in employment contracts that allow some type of defense against surprise attacks.

Contributing to the empowerment of influential members and minority factions is that most church members wish to be courteous. Church observers often note that churches encourage people to be polite rather than effective. People wish to come together peaceably in the presence of God. This is an admirable notion.

Unfortunately, an upshot of being overly courteous is that congregations too often tolerate, and do not confront, inappropriate behavior from forceful personalities. The great fear is that someone will get angry and leave the church. I believe many churches would be better off if this actually happened from time to time.

Ending on a positive note

Whatever the makeup of the committee, I don't believe members should plunge into their checklist of tasks at the first meeting. Many search committee members told me how important that it was to pray together. I strongly urge committee members to take the time to become acquainted, to share their hopes and dreams, their doubts and fears.

A former search committee chair wonderfully articulated the importance of taking time and not rushing into the task, when he wrote:

> *"I would assert that this is, indeed, a neglected area. There are important things that could be done when committee members are relaxed, eager to learn, and before the mechanics of the process overtake any chance for in-depth preparation. Some of the preparatory matters include: introduction to spiritual discernment between a candidate and*

a committee as contrasted with an over-reliance on a numerical scoring process; team building and trust building; ways for the committee chair to earn the confidence of the committee members; taking the time to insist on clear, written expectations of the committee's deliverables and negotiated duration with the parish' governing body; and building an awareness of surprises, pitfalls, and bumps in the road."

It's also important that committees set some ground rules regarding disagreements, different points of view, and how people of varying personality traits can work together effectively over a long period of time. It is also essential to clarify what happens if some committee members really like Pastor Smith and others really like Pastor Anderson.

It is entirely appropriate for the search committee to ask for the resources and the expertise they need, at any phase of the process. This includes bringing in a judicatory representative or outside consultant. Doing so is not an admission of failure, but rather a genuine desire for the process to be successful.

The worst thing that can happen is for a search committee to choose a candidate because members are worn to a frazzle and want to get it over with. This is sometimes called the exhaustion cycle, and tends to occur in later stages when search committees have difficulty narrowing the field or choosing between two good candidates.[7]

Let's end this chapter with a wonderful example of how the search committee can provide the ministerial candidate a metaphorical map of the congregation. With this map in hand, the new minister will know the location of:

Wells (people who are sources of refreshments)
Food (people who feed the soul)
Banks (people who have critical resources)
Fire hydrants (people who put out fires)
Schools (people who have important information for you)
Priests (people who will keep confidence)
Grapevines (people who broadcast information)
Museums (people who have the history)
Safety patrols (those who know where the land mines are)[8]

I'd also add the previous pastors "in-group" and "out-group." These are people who were particularly close to the minister and, conversely, those who had the most difficulty with the pastor. The current in-group might assume they will continue their role with the new pastor. Those in the out-group may wish to seize upon a new opportunity. Not all may be satisfied in their new roles.

Speaking of new roles, a word to the wise for the newly settled minister. Be keenly aware of church members who are the first to schedule appointments. These souls may be among the most needy and the most problematic. They are also likely to have issues or agendas, which they may pursue whether the new minister is supportive or not.

As we've seen, there are some tricky maneuvers in the search process, and in the new minister getting settled. I'm hoping your experience on the search committee is one of great joy, spiritual discovery, deeply profound friendships, a minister who is thrilled to be headed your way, and a new vision of your church's future.

CHAPTER 9

Not Everyone Tells the Truth

"Search committees often have wild expectations of their church's potential."
— A Synod official who works in ministerial settlement

Some years ago I worked with a congregation that faced some challenges that are all too familiar in mainline Protestantism. Membership was on a plateau, the pledge drive barely covered expenses, the leadership was cautious, outreach was minimal, and the church lacked direction. My report reflected these issues, and contained various recommendations regarding how to proceed. I didn't view this church as unhealthy, but rather drifting aimlessly along.

The following year, the minister retired and the church went into search. I was quite surprised when I received their congregational profile in the mail. It was mostly sweetness and light, with a great deal of flowery language about the future. The congregational survey indicated their primary desire was for an excellent preacher. Little of what I had addressed in my report was contained in the profile.

Church members believed the description of their congregation was largely accurate. The church was a clean, well-lighted place, the leadership communicated few of the congregation's problems, income from a modest endowment covered occasional budget shortfalls, a small number of dedicated volunteers kept the place running, there was little urgency about anything in particular, and church members were quite comfortable with the way things were.

It seems to be common knowledge among ministers that church profiles rarely convey a complete accounting of a church's true situation. It's not that well-intentioned church folk are disingenuous. Rather, a large percentage of congregants are not "in the know" with scant awareness of the church's actual state of affairs.

In most parishes, only about twenty percent of members have a reasonably accurate understanding of the church's true circumstances. In other words, four out of five don't. This is a major reason why church profiles resemble those chipper family Christmas letters that filter out every hint of difficulty or struggle.

I've also discovered that even among the twenty percent who comprehend the congregation's true situation, few have read any church literature, and are unversed in the nature and character of the religious communities they serve. I find this a peculiar phenomenon. Church leaders are educated people, and if they are curious about any given subject, from backyard birds to stars in the sky to a particular historical era, they have ready access to a wide range of resources to answer their questions.

But upon being appointed to a church board or other leadership role, this curiosity seems to end. People automatically assume they know how to perform the task at hand. I'm familiar with search committees that boasted they didn't need a consultant or outside help. They would make it up on their own.

Most church leaders bring their secular experience to a community of faith, and sometimes this translates but most often it does not. Few grasp the detrimental effects that a rapidly changing world has had on their congregations, and the challenges that lie ahead.

It's perfectly understandable that congregations put on their happiest faces. As we will see, this "good news" scenario illustrates two important issues in the search for a minister. The first, as we've seen, is the tendency of churches to understate problematic issues. The second is that ministers can be seduced into thinking they have the potential to lead a congregation that presents only garden- variety concerns. Let's take a look at each of these in turn.

Glossing over unhappy details

Many churches fit the above, all is well, description. Church leaders don't want anything to go wrong, and wish to keep members unruffled. If no conflict arises, churches like this can roll along quite adequately. This is particularly the case with family and pastoral-sized congregations of 200 members or fewer. Congregations of this size are the most resistant to change.

When in search, small churches may seek a minister who is "one of us," who will blend into the woodwork and congregational life continues on as before. The hidden message is "nurture us, but don't challenge us." Or, "we don't need leadership."[1]

Many church members also desire their congregations to be one big happy family. They prefer simplicity over complexity, and don't wish to squabble with fellow parishioners over matters large or small. Predictability and familiarity are valued traits of congregational life. Why fix something that isn't broken? Why change things all around?

In turn, many ministers desire to serve peaceful, settled-in congregations, as they wish to preach and provide pastoral care to their flocks. An appropriate metaphor is a kindly shepherd and a flock of well-cared-for sheep. I dwell on this particular church because most congregations in America have 250 members or fewer.

However, a major drawback to small and pastoral-sized churches is the tendency to remain on membership plateaus, as members become older and grayer. Churches of this size often lose the ability to reach out to younger generations. The congregational life that people grasp so tightly creates a reticence to change that actually sabotages the future of the church they love so dearly.[2]

The situation is very different in larger congregations. The issues are more complex, more immediate, and the pace of congregational life is much quicker. Larger churches are characterized by "multiple points of entry." This means a wider array of congregational programs; more members with particular skills and talents they wish to utilize; a need for highly skilled clergy, staff, and lay leaders; a need for more timely and accurate communications; and a more significant role for the finance committee.

A larger church's complexity also raises the bar in terms of the accuracy of the congregation's profile, and the qualifications and expertise of members of the search committee.

Everyone is on their best behavior

In the search process, both churches and ministers wish to put their best feet forward. But human nature being what it is, people have their quirks, biases, and blind spots.

For example, members of the search committee may range in age from their twenties to their eighties. Younger members may be completely unaware of church struggles that linger in the memories of longer-term parishioners.

As mentioned, search committee members may be unfamiliar with pressing issues within the church. For example, I'm familiar with one church in which committees functioned like personal fiefdoms. Many committees met at parishioners' homes, didn't announce meeting times or dates, didn't keep records, and rarely recruited new members. They felt no accountability to the church board, or to anyone, for that matter.

When the new minister arrived, she appropriately inquired about reporting relationships and accountability. Some committee chairs were highly defensive. The minister became viewed, incorrectly, as being heavy-handed, and found herself enmeshed in difficulties not of her making.

I recall another congregation whose current board chair was the eighth choice, and a very poor selection. The board was in a state of disarray, yet board members were reluctant to mention this outside their own ranks because it would reflect poorly on them. When board members rotated off, their lips were sealed.

The search committees in both churches just mentioned didn't realize that lay leaders behaved in this manner, and didn't mention these issues to candidates. This created two identical problems: the search committee didn't realize how difficult it was to recruit leadership for key roles, and the congregation had no plan to address such serious issues.

I don't blame search committees for this state of affairs. Their intentions are highly honorable, and they might have requested a thorough explanation of the church's situation. But church church leaders may have succumbed to the temptation to paint a portrait of a congregation that was more hopeful than realistic.

For instance, the board chair might have said, "We've had some leadership problems, but we're working through them." Or, a staff member may have reported, "Recruiting Sunday school teachers is difficult, but we're formulating a plan to address that." A few church members may have said, "For the past fifteen years, this church has always wanted to do X,Y, or Z, and with a new minister, we can surely realize this." The chair of the Buildings and Grounds committee added, "The congregation needs to address deferred maintenance of the building, and surely members will support a capital campaign to accomplish this."

So the search committee presents this congregational perspective to ministerial candidates in good faith. But when push comes to shove, if that new idea is not in the budget, it will not come to pass. The leadership problem, vaguely defined, may or may not be addressed. The plan for recruiting Sunday school teachers may or may not be effective. There may be some hesitancy to conduct a capital campaign if economic conditions aren't right.

All these issues are presented to the candidate as being well in hand, when in fact, they are systemic weaknesses lying in wait for the incoming minister to deal with. This results in a common complaint among ministers, that search committees water down the expectations of the job. Once hired, the congregation expects the minister to address a wide range of issues that were not identified during the interview process.[3]

The minister's role in the scheme of things

By nature, most ministers are extraordinarily honest, conscientious people, and parishioners trust them with their hearts and souls. But like anyone looking for a new job, ministers may also adopt their own rosy, Christmas-letter approach to presenting their credentials.

Obviously, ministers emphasize their good points, which may be many, varied, and exceptional. However, they're not likely to mention occasional sermons containing political references that got them in hot water. They might pass over an occasional forgetfulness about returning phone calls, or their habit of spending too much time online with their personal blogs. After all, these aren't really important, make-it-or-break it issues, are they? Is anyone's spiritual life in jeopardy?

I believe that living in a minor state of denial is a very good thing. Doing so helps us pretend that life's scary things either don't exist or will never happen to us. But ministers who overstate their qualifications in the search process will not find this to be an asset. For example, the search committee of a cathedral church received over 100 applications for the role of Dean of the Cathedral. On examination, less than ten were qualified to serve a church of 1,400 members whose physical plant occupied an entire downtown city block. Part of me admires the ninety who gave it a shot, but we do need to be realistic.

Ministers in search sometimes experience what is called the "halo effect." This is the tendency to see any church as they want it to be, either in terms of being better than it really is, or in terms of possessing the particular characteristics they are seeking. The problem with the halo effect is that its intensity seems to increase in direct proportion to a minister's need to receive a new call.[4]

The expectations of the minister are very high

I recently spoke with the chair of a search committee about what type of minister the church wished to call. I reviewed the credentialing process for ministers in some denominations that encompass fifteen or more areas of expertise. These include worship, preaching, Biblical literacy, management, finance, administration, fundraising, evangelism, knowledge of youth and adult religious development, Christian education, teaching, pastoral care, visitation ministries, community ministries, and worldwide social concerns.

One denomination recently added knowledge of sexual development and sexual disorders, and another produced a checklist of 32 areas of "giftedness in ministry" in which ministers were to rate themselves. I've also seen ministerial evaluation forms in one church or another, in which parishioners are asked to rate the minister's performance in 43 different areas.

Added to this list are personal attributes that ministers are to embody, such as a deep and growing personal faith, relating well to people, being self-aware, possessing a positive leadership style, being organized, open to new learning, living with integrity, maintaining self-control, and having good health, energy, and enthusiasm.

One denomination's resource guide for search committees listed 147 questions that can be asked of ministerial candidates. Whew! Just reading all this makes me tired.

I asked the search committee chair whether they could find a minister who could meet all these criteria, and if not, which areas might receive less emphasis. He replied, "We expect to find a minister who embodies most of the above."

One observer listed the expectations of the minister as, "He must be sinless, he must be constantly available, he must be capable of meeting every need, he must have no spiritual or emotional needs himself, and he must never let on that he has any material need."[5]

These standards, often institutionalized by denominational offices, are vastly unrealistic. Yet clergy, search committees, and congregations buy into this system. With all these skills and attributes floating about in

the ether of denominational norms, how do ministers and search committees prioritize their talking points?

The next two chapters address these, and a number of other related
issues.

CHAPTER 10

Money in the Church

*"Never consider a church seriously until you have
a crystal clear idea of its finances."*
— Excellent advice from church observers too numerous to mention

M inisters sometimes claim they know little about church finance
and may want to skip the subject entirely. Please don't. Your
compensation package, pension, financial well-being, and the
health of your congregation depend on informed ministerial leadership.

Ministers of all denominations should be aware that ignorance of
church finance is an Achilles' heel of colossal proportion. If you're unfamiliar with basic budgeting procedures, take a course in nonprofit finance
or find a kindly soul who will bring you up to speed. If you don't understand the financial conversation, you'll be out of the loop. Your leadership
in a decisive area of congregational life will be severely diminished.

Where to begin

The annual operating budget is one of the most informative documents the congregation will provide. Truer words were never spoken
than, "For where your treasure is, there your heart will be also." (Matthew
6:21)

If you're unfamiliar with the traditional line item budget, a rudi-
mentary glance and some basic arithmetic will reveal many important,
need-to-know facts. Let's begin with acquiring not just the current year's
operating budget, but copies of the budget for the past five years.

As of this writing, the past three years have been extremely difficult
economically for churches of all faiths. Decreasing pledge income, staff
cutbacks, and reductions in programming are the norm. Few churches

have gone unscathed, and it is essential to compare five years of budget figures to learn where cuts have been made. It is critically important to understand not only where cuts occurred, but also how the church leadership made some hard decisions.

It is also imperative to determine if church leaders have resigned themselves to cutting back for the foreseeable future. This is because a church that does less may not translate into a minister who does less. In fact, working with limited resources, and with parishioners who are struggling financially and may be demoralized, is considerably more difficult than conducting ministry in good times.

Do church leaders believe they are more or less ineffectual, waiting on the sidelines for better times? Or, will those same leaders be proactive in addressing the church's financial condition. Will leaders plan a supplemental pledge drive? Will they host a special event that raises money to halt further cuts or restore a previous level of service? Will they ask the most affluent members to make special gifts?

Let me provide an example. I began working with an Episcopal church shortly after the October, 2008 stock market crash. In a series of discussions, the leadership felt this would be the worst possible time to cut back, with so many people in obvious need. The vestry (the church board) agreed to give away the offering each Sunday, and planned a comprehensive, every-member pledge drive. A year later, plate offerings had increased from $5,000 to $20,000, and the pledge drive increased by 12 percent. This is a church of 190 members in a neighborhood of modestly priced homes.

Ministers need to know if they will be coming to a congregation in which inevitability is the defining factor, or to a congregation that believes it can control its destiny. The success of your ministry swings in the balance.

An essential measure of a congregation's character

Next, examine carefully the line item in the budget for mission and outreach beyond the congregation's four walls. This line item should be separate from denominational or diocesan dues. Mission and outreach is a significant indicator of a congregation's heart and soul, its attitude toward money, and what the congregation feels called to do in this place and time.

Allow me to dispel one myth right now—that affluent congregations have ample funds and healthy attitudes toward money. In my experience, some of the most troubled congregations are in upscale communities, or have the largest endowments. One minister in a church with a substantial endowment told me, "I don't have a congregation, I have a group of private investors. They act as though the endowment is their own money. When the stock market takes a dive, they sweat bullets, thinking the endowment should pay for everything, fearing they might be asked to make up the difference."

Another minister lamented, "I have a wealthy congregation of stingy givers. In the midst of great wealth, money is always short and we fight over it constantly. These arguments drain us of the energy to carry out God's will in the world."

Getting back to mission and outreach,

> *The amount of money a church commits to creating a more just and humane world reveals a congregation's character more than any other factor. If a congregation is miserly in its outreach, it will be miserly in everything else it does.*

I'm taken aback by parishioners in comfortable, middle-class churches who say, "We can't afford to do any of that. We need to take care of ourselves first." As if they weren't taken care of already.

Such congregations do not have a face (or a heart) turned toward the outside world, but rather an inward focus, toward their own members. They mainly raise money for themselves. If the line item for mission is zero, or not even included on the budget form, ministers should look elsewhere. In a miserly church, your ministry will be death by a thousand cuts.

For example, I worked with a congregation that was debating the extent of outreach they could accomplish. I recommended the board set a small percentage, perhaps three percent of the budget. This decision was within their rightful authority. Against my advice, church leaders introduced the idea of committing one percent at the annual meeting, and called for a vote. The measure eventually passed, but the discussion was heated and some left angry. One penny on the dollar! As we have seen throughout this book, old customs, even those that limit the ministry of the congregation, die slowly. Here was an opportunity to serve the world that turned into a church fight. The Holy Spirit didn't have a chance.

If ministerial candidates discover low-level giving toward outreach and mission, do not be mislead by comments that various groups fund their own outreach efforts that are "off budget." Or, that church members pay for things from their own pockets that aren't accounted for. These may be true, but are sidetracks to avoid the larger subject.

One exception to this rule involves a church I'm familiar with that supports a hospital in Haiti. Throughout the year, doctors, dentists, and healthcare professionals volunteer days and weeks of their time, with many individual congregants paying the lion's share of the costs beyond what they pledge to the church. This is a soul-stirring ministry that serves some of the most desperately poor people on the face of the earth.

Of course, not every congregation has this capacity. But small-dollar, short-term, piecemeal mission efforts within shouting distance of your church building do not touch the heart and will not strengthen your congregation's resolve to do right by the world. Such attitudes only weaken your church's ability to accomplish anything of significance, or to reach your congregation's full potential.

In addition, don't be taken in by the claim that church members give their time instead of their money. This also may be true, but churches need members' time and their money. There's no getting around it. Of course, people who are struggling financially get a bye. But there's a human need to give, and all should contribute in proportion to what they have received. Charity is enjoined upon us all, not just those who are perceived to afford it.

Most congregations claim they are generous, but many are not. Church leaders, and possibly search committee members, may put themselves through contortions attempting to shore up their congregation's lack of generosity. I believe all churches should include at least a 10 percent line item in the budget for mission and outreach. This line item should come first, and funds should be distributed as the church year progresses, not at the end of the year if there is cash left over.

Ministerial candidates should insist on the congregation striving to reach this goal because the healthiest and happiest congregations give away a larger than average share to mission and outreach.

The ultimate example is the Memorial Drive Presbyterian Church in Houston, Texas. This church gives one dollar to the needs of the world for every dollar it spends on itself. This is a line item of 100 percent for mission. In stark contrast, the aforementioned church that argued about one percent for mission is a church that deprives people of joy and hardens their hearts to those less fortunate. Just the opposite of what churches should do.

Pledge records

Ministerial candidates should request a summary of gifts and pledges, from highest to lowest, for the past five years. Database programs can easily print these records, with or without names attached. Make sure the list contains non-donor households.

Many churches do not concern themselves with non-donors, and some database programs do not include them if a gift amount is not recorded. *This is an extremely important fact to know, especially if the number of non-donor households is growing.* I worked with a church in which 12 percent of members were non-donors. Is this fact unimportant?

Once on the job, ministers should receive the gift and pledge records of all church members. Ministers are often advised they should not review gift records because of potential favoritism toward those who give the most. I have found this not to be true. In my experience, the most generous donors don't ask for special favors. They give far more than they ask in return.

However, at the bottom end of the pledge list, you may discover that an inordinate number of complaints, petty gripes, and requests for special favors come from those who give the least. Ministers need current pledge information, to consider the source.

Ministers should also review gift records when considering people for leadership roles. The last person you want in a key role is a low-level donor from a high-income household. That person will be first in line to say the church should not attempt new ministries because the money isn't there, and the congregation certainly cannot be asked to give more. On that subject, a church board with a majority of low-level donors is a liability and not an asset. Access to the pledge records is an essential tool for effective ministry.

Ministers should also be kept apprised of pledge payments on a quarterly basis. Sometimes, parishioners pledge a certain dollar amount but because of financial difficulties may not be able to pay that pledge. Some people become embarrassed by their inability to fulfill a pledge, and stop coming to church. This is the time they need the church the most. If the minister doesn't know congregants are struggling because he or she hasn't been informed, what purpose is served? A healing ministry goes undone.

I suspect that secrecy surrounding pledge figures is the result of church leaders who were low-level donors and didn't want anyone to find out. This as an institutionalized bad habit, which unfortunately can date back decades in time.

In requesting the full range of pledge figures, do not settle for the average pledge alone, a figure that may be in the range of $2,500. The average pledge calculation conveys the idea that everyone in the church pledges the about same amount. In actuality, the average pledge is often grossly distorted, due to a small number of very large pledges at the top and the omission of non-donor households at the bottom.

A more accurate calculation is the median pledge, half above and half below. A church claiming the average pledge is $2,500 may have a median pledge of $600. Thus, half the membership gives barely more than $10 per week.

Ministers should not be deterred in seeking this information with reasons such as difficulty in obtaining it from the computer system, or because the giving records are known only by the treasurer. In my experience, the higher the secrecy, the lower the charitable giving.

Once the figures are in hand, you may be unpleasantly surprised at what you see. You may find that 30 percent of the congregation gives 70 percent of the total. This is called a giving pyramid, or skewed giving, and it exists in all congregations. The more important factor is the angle of the pyramid. The steeper the angle, the more dependent the church will be on a small number of donors.

I worked with a mid-sized congregation in which three donor households each contributed $30,000 annually. All were in their eighties. Once they had passed away, it required approximately sixty "average" pledges of $1,500 to make up the difference. The church became over-reliant on these three families, and it took about five years to recover $90,000 in lost pledges, including some painful cuts along the way.

Also look at the number of donors at certain giving levels. For example, donors at $10,000 and above; $5,000 to $10,000; $2,500 to $5,000; $1,000 to $2,500; and below $1,000. The number of donors increases as the gift size decreases. The large number of donors at the bottom may have little correlation with household income.

You may find the "mode," the most frequent number of pledges of the same amount, at $1,200, $600, and $300. This is $100 monthly, $50 monthly, and $25 monthly, respectively. Church members may have pledged these same amounts for years on end. With many mainline churches located in middle-class neighborhoods, it is highly improbable that someone giving $25 monthly could not afford $50. Or that someone giving $50 could not afford $100. Yet again, old habits die hard, like one-dollar bills in the collection plate.

One last time, most middle class parishioners could double their charitable giving to all causes, and not notice the slightest difference in their daily lives. Literally, your congregation could double its annual pledge drive with ease. Why not go for it, seize the moment?

Beyond pledge figures

Most small to medium-sized churches have fairly simple budgets that contain the figures on income and expenses. The amounts for personnel and benefits are straightforward, and committees are likely to receive relatively small amounts of money for their work. These numbers add up in a fairly clear-cut manner, and should be simple to interpret. Still, if you need help walking through the budget, ask for it.

However, some churches own rental property, have a variety of endowed funds, carry outstanding debt, calculate depreciation, and require significantly more complex financial statements. For the uninitiated, these financial statements are like reading Greek. Ministers may be challenged to gain a grasp of the financial reports that look so daunting, but you must persevere. Do not throw up your hands and say it's all above your head.

Another key financial factor

Ministerial candidates need to be fully aware of any debt the church carries, and the terms for payment of such obligations. The operating budget will list monthly debt payments, but not the percentage of interest paid and length of the term.

Find out what the terms are, because the bank always gets paid first.

Some congregations carry loans that have balloon payments. This is a chunk of money, sometimes a big chunk, that is due at the end of a specified loan period. If that payment is ten years out, congregations can become nonchalant that a balloon payment looms out there, and panic when the due date approaches because they don't have the money to pay it. Churches are then forced to renew the loan, sometimes under less favorable terms.

If debt exists, an important question a ministerial candidate should ask is whether the leadership will initiate a debt-reduction campaign. In many congregations, there's no need to pay sizable amounts of interest and carrying charges, sometimes for decades. Launching a capital campaign will appeal to conservatives, as this is fiscally responsible and saves money; and to liberals, as that money can be put to much better use in the community. A win-win for all!

Different kinds of money

If a high percentage of the congregation's income derives from member pledges, the leadership needs to ensure that highly skilled parishioners manage the annual pledge drive. Your congregation's goal, outlined in the concept of membership in good standing, is to encourage members to reach the 5-10 percent giving level as soon as possible.

If this happens, the church will have plenty of money and won't have to conduct the annual pledge drive at all. For most congregations, this will be a blessing and a relief. As a friend of mine once said, "The annual pledge drive in this church is like a congregational root canal."

If your church continues to use the annual pledge drive format, the best advice I can offer is not to place the operating budget as the centerpiece. Author Ashley Hale writes, "Almost all budgets are compromised, watered-down documents. The average budget provides no reason for generous giving and countless excuses for token giving. It is at best hesitant and fearful and at worst static and apologetic."[1] Each line item is the opportunity for church members to say, "Why do we have to spend so much money on…" Often, this starts with the minister's compensation. In too many instances, the budget is a disincentive to charitable giving.

Philanthropy is a way of life, not paying bills. Anyone of any means can become a philanthropist. This is the business churches should be in.

Rental and endowment income

A few simple calculations will reveal what percentage of the budget comes from annual giving, and what percentage comes from renting space or other sources. High rental income, perhaps from a school or daycare center on site, may create a reliance on that income and result in low-level giving among congregants. I once worked with a church that derived $675,000 in annual revenue from a parking lot. Church members gave a pittance. How in the world can people develop a spiritual life if they are miserly in their hearts?

Next, does the church have an endowment? If so, what is the principal amount, how is the money invested, and who makes investment decisions? If the endowment is not a sizeable amount, an investment committee of church members may determine the makeup of the portfolio. If the endowment involves serious money, that job may be contracted to an outside investment firm.

An especially important issue is whether interest income from the endowment is used to supplement the annual operating budget. Similar to rental or parking lot income, interest from an endowment can create a low-pledging congregation that becomes overly dependent on outside monies.

Since many endowments exist because of memorial gifts, taking interest income for current operations is sometimes gruesomely referred to as living off dead people's money. A friend of mine coined a little ditty about his church that goes, "Free, free, everything's free. We're fully endowed through the next century."

The use of endowment income for current operations may be a matter of conscience among some congregants. They believe the endowment was never intended to give current-day parishioners a low-cost ride. Others argue that the money's there, so why not use it. Attempting to wean a congregation off manna from heaven is not a task for the faint of heart. Why should members pay more for something they get for less? Ministers can broach the subject, but any initiative to reduce dependency on outside monies needs to be a congregation-wide, collaborative effort.

Taking interest from the endowment is the reason why some congregations set up independent foundations that are outside the governance of the church. Usually, the first bylaw in the foundation's charter is that interest income from the endowment may not supplement the operating budget of the congregation.

An organization called Partners for Sacred Places (www.sacred-places.org) has helped many congregations preserve downtown historic churches through the formation of foundations. Donors who are interested in historic preservation may not be members of the church or even subscribe to its theology. Nevertheless, they recognize the historical importance of the building, and want to preserve the structure as part of the city's heritage.

The minister's compensation package

Churches can live longer without ministers than ministers can live without compensation. The church has the great advantage in the decision-making process.[2] Candidates may feel the church has the upper hand regarding compensation issues, as well.

Most denominations now utilize recommended salary guidelines, often based on the size of the congregation and the number of years of experience the minister carries. These guidelines have improved the financial lot of countless clergy families. However, not all churches meet salary guidelines, and in my experience, pleas to the congregation to increase clergy and staff compensation through increased charitable giving usually fall on deaf ears.

If clergy begin working for less, they will continue working for less. Most Protestant churchgoers, sadly, give between one and two percent of their incomes to the church. This equates into incremental increases in compensation being the best a minister can hope for. Sometimes these small increases are granted grudgingly.

On the subject of salaries, candidates might keep in mind that some churches wish to call a younger minister to follow a more experienced minister, so the church can save money on the compensation package. Of course, the responsibilities of the new minister remain the same or grow larger, as the younger person is expected to be more energetic and get more accomplished. One search committee suggested that a single pastor would have more time to devote to the church and require less of a social life, so that pastor wouldn't need to be paid as much. As the humorist Dave Barry would say, "I am not making this up."

Finally, regarding your compensation package and other financial issues, do not assume competence on the part of those negotiating for the church. Contract negotiation may be an unfamiliar subject. Make sure every detail is clearly defined, and the fine print carefully understood. Your local judiciary official may be especially helpful in this regard.

For example, I read an anecdote about a church having a sabbatical fund. The minister assumed the money was for his use, to pursue additional study or sabbatical plans. Seven years later, when he came to his planned leave, he discovered that church leaders believed the money was for visiting preachers in his absence, and other expenses at the church due to his being away.

Another minister discovered that the books she had purchased with the professional expense allocation in her compensation package were viewed as being the property of the church's library, and not her own.

A few closing comments

This is not a book on stewardship, but then again, it is. If a congregation lives out its call to ministry, money should be a secondary concern. If it's the right thing to do, the money will be there.

Charitable giving is one of God's greatest gifts to us mortals here on earth. When we sit down to write a check to the church or to an organization that holds great meaning for us, that should be one of those "ahh" moments – life as good as it gets. Many people claim they feel the closest to God when doing this.

I'd like to close this chapter with some words from Robert Wuthnow, Director of the Center for the Study of American Religion at Princeton University. He is a strong advocate for the church playing a more significant role in American life today. His words further the theme of this book, that courageous voices are needed on many fronts.

> *"Clergy lament the materialization of our society and the pressures to work harder and spend more. They worry that young people are being corrupted by false and misleading values of the marketplace. They acknowledge that wealth and generosity do not go hand in hand. Most clergy realize there is theological support for these opinions. Still, they find it hard to say anything that might seem to criticize the ways their parishioners are living."*[3]

These are such powerful words, and such a powerful vision of what the church, and all of us, should be called to do.

CHAPTER 11

Power and Authority in the Church

"Many power lines run through the church, and it may be tricky
figuring out which ones carry the highest voltage."
— Peter Raible

I t's an odd thing. Groups that have legitimate power, like church
boards, rarely use it. Individuals and assorted groups that are granted
no justifiable power use it whenever they wish.

Throughout this chapter, we'll discuss the difference between power
and authority in the church. We'll also observe how various characters in
the drama play out their roles on stage. Let's begin with the leadership.

The church board

In my consulting practice, I've worked with about 100 congregations
and thus, 100 church boards. Most of these boards assumed their rightful
authority over the budget process, monitoring of expenses, and oversight
of committee work. They kept current with myriad issues regarding
administration, finance, care of the property, and ongoing church
programs. They fielded occasional complaints. Most board members did
reasonably well with these issues because that's their traditional role, and
what their predecessors did.

As author Aubrey Malphurs notes, "Most church boards operate on
the basis of informed tradition. New members come on board and
observe the culture of the current board and the role it plays. They
become acculturated, function in the same ways, and the situation perpet-
uates itself, without challenge.[1]

As previously noted, most people coming onto church boards don't
feel a need for additional education, training, or expertise to fulfill their

roles. Nor does the church provide much. An annual board retreat might be scheduled, but these usually involve current board members discussing congregational life, and are not educational in nature. Sometimes, denominations host leadership events, which can be informative. At the same time, these programs can be inconsistent and generic in nature, or reflect established beliefs.

One astute observer noted that church boards tend to believe there's a narrow range of decisions they can make, but everything outside this range is prohibited. I have found this to be largely true.

The most significant power that boards exercise is the firing of an employee, sometimes the minister. In some denominations, boards cannot even do this without approval from the bishop or a higher governing body. Church boards also exhibit their power by nixing new ideas that come along, even modest ideas, usually because there's no money in the budget.

So if I pulled out my voltmeter and took a reading, it would give church boards a high rating in authority and a low rating in power, except for their heightened power to stop new ideas.

Shouldn't it be just the opposite? That church boards should have a plentiful dose of positive power to begin new ministries, rather than their primary strength being negative power, to halt new ideas. This voltmeter reading also applies to most committees, as well.

This aspect of power in the church can be illustrated as follows:

When someone proposes a new idea, decide how it should be handled. If you want it rejected, refer it to a standing committee. If you decide it needs refining and improving, send it to a special study committee. If it has obvious merit and deserves to be implemented, create a special ad hoc committee and direct its members to turn that proposal into reality.[2]

An example of a powerful ad hoc group is a capital campaign committee for a big-ticket building renovation project. Once the idea gets congregational approval, this committee has the authority to define the scope of the work, set a dollar goal for the campaign, raise the money, hire an architect, engage a contractor, pay invoices, and oversee the project as a whole. If the task unfolds without major glitches, the capital campaign committee will receive minimal oversight from the board. The voltmeter for the capital campaign committee reads high in unquestioned power and authority.

Sometimes church members view power in the church as a bad thing. This is not the case at all. Of course, some people abuse the power they claim, which we'll discuss in a moment. But for now, in addition to the campaign committee just mentioned, we might also include influential groups that begin new outreach initiatives, or revamp the visitation program for sick or elderly members.

Nothing happens in church unless someone is in charge.

Determining how power flows through the church may be difficult to discern. When I work with a congregation, the first session I hold is with the leadership, and I ask the minister and board chair to define who falls into this category. Usually, 25-30 people show up. Most are current or former board members, or committee chairs, the recognized leaders. But on numerous occasions, someone has said to me, "The people who make the real decisions are not in the room."

Some church members believe that influential congregants call the shots, and this exercise of power is a bad thing as well. Perhaps, but perhaps not. Influential members may, in fact, be a congregation's greatest asset.

I've met countless dedicated, committed souls who give inordinate amounts of time, effort, and money to the church. They are often among the church's largest donors, and are always there when a need arises. Some are respected elders, those "weighty souls" as the Quakers claim, who give churches an unmistakable character. They are the living saints. They have no interest in seeking power or authority in the church because they already possess ample portions of both in their personal or professional lives.

On the other hand

All human institutions have influential players, and in any church, a small cadre of members can make something happen, or prevent something from happening. Ministerial candidates need to know whether the church is inordinately influenced by one group or another, for better or worse. We've just seen a few examples of the better.

But in many congregations, a ubiquitous minority always seems to have a beef about something or other. Some congregants shrug and say, "Oh, that's Joe and his pals," or, "those are just the constant whiners."

Ministers need to understand fully that a small number of people who are persistent in their efforts can become disproportionately powerful and turn a healthy congregation into a dysfunctional one, if permitted to do so. Please note that disruptive personalities are only effective with the complicity of others, including the congregation's leadership.

A friend of mine is a Presbyterian minister, and he met with a group of perennially disgruntled members following a Sunday service. Accompanied by the board chair, he said, "No matter what the church does or what I do, you are increasingly unhappy. I don't believe you perceive the voice of God here anymore, and I'm asking you to take a leave of absence for two years, to ponder and to pray about this."

I believe this was a caring invitation by that minister. In doing so, he helped preserve the health and well-being of the remaining members. It is unfortunate but necessary to point out that some church members are "radioactive" or "toxic" personalities, and seek out those of like mind, like alcoholics who don't want to drink alone.

The late Edwin Friedman wrote extensively about the tendency of leaders in many types of organizations "who believe that toxic forces can be managed through reasonableness, love, insight, role-modeling, and striving for consensus rather than taking stands that limit the invasiveness of those who lack self-regulation."[3] Friedman also added his belief that continual attempts to achieve consensus will leverage power to the extremists.

Inappropriate behavior should not be tolerated under any circumstances. Sadly, I've worked with congregations in which the minister and key leaders were actually fearful of certain groups. It's not always a matter of vocal pushback. Sometimes, it's the threat of leaving the church and withdrawing financial support. If people threaten to leave, let them go. Do not, under any circumstances, chase after them and bring them back. If they return, they will have the fury of 10,000 suns. Be forewarned that a sizable amount of negative, concentrated power can drive a congregation to ruin.

The power of the congregation

In faith traditions that function on the basis of congregational polity, "the congregation" is the ultimate arbiter. But if most aspects of church life proceed relatively smoothly, members of the congregation tend to be fairly tranquil. And why not? Why make a fuss about minor matters?

However, a congregation can react with rage if they believe they've been excluded from a significant decision. Take personnel issues, for example. I know two ministers who were forced out of their congregations because they fired a staff member. When a staff member is terminated, it is the business of only a few people: the employee, his or her supervisor, and the church board.

But as one church observer notes, "Yet it's common for all sorts of people in a congregation to think it's their business and insert themselves into the situation even though it's against the law to discuss an employee's record or performance. When this happens, serious problems can become crises."

He continues, "Sometimes congregations do business the way six-year-olds play soccer - they play 'bunch ball.' Everyone runs to the ball. Everyone has to be in on every decision. No one plays his or her position. It doesn't work in soccer and it doesn't work in church governance. Being a good church member means knowing which tasks and business have your name on it, and which ones don't. It involves a respect for the roles that help govern a congregation and not overstepping them."[4]

However, a long-standing tradition in many churches is that "all voices should be heard." The theory is that a good decision will derive from the members' collective voices. I disagree. I've been involved in many congregational discussions, and not all voices are informed voices. Many, in fact, are quite erroneous, and act against the best interests of the congregation as a whole.

I once heard a church leader say the minister's salary should be reduced because the minister wanted to begin small group ministry, and this would deplete the volunteer pool. This would be laughable if it wasn't so very tragic.

Church members should certainly involve themselves when a congregational vote is required. The two most legitimate occasions are calling a new minister and approving a capital campaign, as these decisions require congregational input. Beyond these two significant decisions in the life of a congregation, the leadership should resolve most matters.

Two unfortunate possibilities can result in holding congregational votes. The first is that innovative ideas rarely result from a majority vote. Most often, congregational votes reinforce the status quo. The second reason, more perilous, is the vote may come in at 52 - 48 percent. This means that half the congregation ends up on the losing side of the issue, an unsettling resolution that may carry long-term consequences.

The power and authority of the minister

In congregations of many faith traditions, I've discovered a widespread fear of the minister with the authoritarian personality. These ministers are often described as wanting to be the king or queen. I've met ministers like this, and I'm continually taken aback by the appearance of such personalities in the church.

I always believed that ministry was about helping people find that spark of the divine, the presence of God within themselves, and using that spark to assist the congregation in creating a more just and humane world. Leadership is all about the redeeming and rebuilding of human lives.

A related perspective is found in Robert Greenleaf's classic book about servant leadership. He writes:

> "The very essence of leadership, going out ahead to show the way, derives from more than usual openness to inspiration. Why would anyone accept the leadership of another except that the other sees more clearly where it is best to go? And the issue is not always what we want, but what is being asked of us?[5]

Unfortunately, I have found authoritarian ministers too seldom use their influence to inspire and lead, but rather to keep everyone in their places. I don't often find a ministerial display of blatant authority. Rather, it often appears as a type of passive-aggressive micromanagement, overseeing every aspect of congregational life. Church boards can function in this manner, as well.

I suspect the minister-who-would-be-king does not possess a true call to ministry, misunderstands the nature and character of religious communities, or has unresolved ego issues.

The larger the congregation, the more rightful authority the minister possesses. Even so, the successful large-church ministers I know exercise their authority by including others in the conversation.

> Effective ministers in churches of any size are highly skilled at developing lay leaders who take on significant areas of responsibility. They willingly share power and authority. If you are a minister who is threatened by skilled lay leaders, you will feel constantly under siege.

Of particular importance to ministerial candidates is determining if a congregation truly wants leadership. Be informed that most congregants want a minister whose leadership style is facilitative or collaborative because church people fear "loose cannons" running around and want to make sure everything going on has careful oversight.

Shockingly, one denominational form includes the ministerial leadership choice of "submissive." I believe the worst possible minister, and potentially the most destructive, as Edwin Friedman stated, is someone who is incapable of making well-defined stands.

I've also found the more affluent the community and the more highly educated the congregation, the less they seek ministerial leadership. Parishioners are certainly open to suggestions from the minister, but the unspoken attitude is often, "We're smart, capable, and don't need direction. Especially from a newcomer."

In decades past, and perhaps even today, some churches believe the minister is responsible for the spiritual matters of the congregation, while lay leaders oversee temporal matters. I led a number of seminars at a major seminary, and learned that during the 1980s, the seminary taught students that leadership was a dirty word, and as parish ministers, they should never get involved in it!

In years past, ministers were also told that upon arrival in a new church, they should not change anything for the first 12-18 months. To make changes was viewed as disrespecting those who had worked hard to sustain the church over time. Today, the belief is that if newly settled ministers follow this advice, current patterns of congregational life become even more solidified, and exponentially more difficult to change later on.

The minister, as the new kid on the block, should know that a congregation will test your mettle. Richard Lischer writes of attending a meeting of half a dozen people at a farmer's house in his first settlement, at 2:00 on a Saturday afternoon. "The host said, 'Pastor, would you like a beer?' I paused a moment, then said, 'Sure.' The farmer got one beer out of the refrigerator, opened it, and gave it to me. When I asked if any of the others were having one, the farmer said, 'No. What kind of a man drinks beer at 2:00 in the afternoon?' I had been tested, but didn't know if I had passed or failed."[6]

Defining ministerial authority

One of the most critical issues regarding the role of the minister is rarely mentioned in the search literature. This is the issue of the minister having a written job description. I believe a job description is an essential element of a ministerial call. Otherwise, the minister is responsible for everything.

Authors Walker and Patton underscore the importance of the job description by offering this advice:

"Working with no job description is like living in a house with no doors. There is no meaningful security, and you are exposed to every wind that blows through the congregation. Do not believe that having no job description will allow you to implement your personal priorities. All of the other players have their own priorities, which are as valid to them as yours is to you. And together, they have more power and influence than you do."[7]

I've also heard that if ministers don't have a job description, everyone in the congregation has one for them. This dreadful situation is supported, in part, by the congregational survey. Most surveys, as we've seen, list as many as 40 areas of ministry that church members rank in importance. Because one parishioner ranks a particular aspect of ministerial expertise lower than another, it doesn't mean that aspect disappears from the list. In fact, another parishioner might rank that same area of expertise as very high.

For example, many congregations do not want the minister to be involved in fundraising. I disagree with this point of view, but it's very common. So if the minister only preaches the obligatory, once-a-year stewardship sermon, which members often skip because they believe they've heard it before, and the pledge drive falls short, who is to blame? In part, it's the minister, whose sermons could be more inspiring, or who should be visiting elderly members more often, or who should initiate more mission projects, or who should be bringing in more young families. The list goes on and on. All these things are included in the minister's unofficial, yet very real job description. I know of nothing comparable in the secular work environment.

If the board conducts an annual evaluation of the minister's performance without a job description as the basis, it's likely that the minister's response might be, "I didn't know I was responsible for that, too!" I read of one church that expected the minister to tidy up the church each day and mow the lawn in the summertime, as exercises in humility.

Readers may be expecting a sample job description. The few I've been able to locate are extremely vague, and contain phrases like "keep in close touch with staff members and with all organizations in the church." Or, "the minister is pastor, preacher, enabler, initiator, and guide." What could these possibly mean?

One job description I received from a search committee had a "pared down" summary of responsibilities for the minister. The list included:

Worship and Music
Stewardship
Administration and Organization
Evangelism and Fellowship
Volunteer and Mission Coordination
Christian Education
Mission and Outreach
Pastoral Care

I suspect the fine print may have included "walk on water" and "other duties as specified," just to cover the bases. Sometimes, I wish that job description was as simple as, "The minister defines the spiritual journey we are on. The rest of us join the caravan."

CHAPTER 12

Sex, Dating,
and the Ministerial Family

*"Many congregants prefer the minister to be a man who is
happily married to a woman who does not work outside the home,
volunteers at the church, and spends the rest of her time being
a mother to polite, wholesome children."*
—Pastor Search: A Pulpit and Pew Report

In 1965, a United Methodist minister named Charles Merrill Smith
wrote a satirical and somewhat irreverent book titled, *How to Become
a Bishop Without Being Religious.* Among other aspects of church life, he
addressed the matter of the clerical wife. Some readers may find his
language sexist, but his views reflected the times.

> *A clergyman who remains unmarried for more than a year after
> graduation from seminary is suspected of being abnormal, immoral,
> or chicken. If you want to be a bachelor and a preacher, be prepared
> for a dismal future and renounce now the hope for status, prestige,
> emolument, luxury, and all of the spiritual joys which accompany
> a plush suburban pastorate.*

As for the type of woman a pastor should marry, Smith advises,

> *She must not be beautiful, stylish, or sexy. If she is so lovely as to
> make the ladies of the church feel homely, the minister's prospects
> or a shining career in the church, which otherwise may be bright,
> are dimmed by several thousand candlepower.*

And as for having children, Smith notes,

> *The parson's image depends in part on the inability of the congrega-
> tion to imagine you engaging in sexual intercourse. If they think*

about it at all, they should believe their pastor was only fulfilling his social responsibility of fathering children and that he really didn't enjoy the procedure. It's not easy to believe this, of course, if the pastor's wife has a high wattage look about her.[1]

Surprisingly, some of the attitudes that Smith satirizes remain in place today. A sizable percentage of congregants desire a clergyman with a wife and well-behaved children. This is the stereotype, and many church members are convinced that a young clergy family will attract other young families to the church. There is some truth in this, but the chances of finding the stereotypical clergy family decrease as each day goes by.

Like families in society at large, fewer clergy families reflect the mom, dad, and kids portrait. Clergy families now include those with two moms or with two dads, not to mention numerous other iterations, which we'll review in a moment.

For the most part, people in the pews have little interest in the minister's private life, including his or her sex life, unless something untoward happens and becomes public. But with the arrival of gay and lesbian ministers and the higher incidence of divorce among clergy, search committees are being presented with a wider array of ministerial lifestyles than ever before.

A glimpse into yesteryear

For centuries, the norm was a heterosexual, married man as the pastor. Jane Austen's novels often included a single parson, and the maneuvers that clever women employed to find him a suitable mate, preferably a woman of means so life in the parsonage would be less penurious.

On the American continent, Arthur Dimmesdale and Hester Prynne notwithstanding, churchgoers assumed that young, chaste male clerics married young, chaste maidens, and they lived mostly platonic lives thereafter. One exception is the Puritan minister Jonathan Edwards, whose sermon, Sinners in the Hands of an Angry God, remains well known today. In the early 1700s, Edwards fathered seventeen children. Nevertheless, sex in the clergy household was rarely a subject of discussion, in polite company or otherwise.

Until relatively recently, there was also the assumption that a clergyman and his wife would remain married until their dying days. A stable and enduring clergy marriage was a given.

Changing times

Skipping ahead a couple of centuries, sexual mores changed dramatically in the 1960s with the arrival of the birth control pill and the women's liberation movement. Still, sexuality and the clergy family was not a particularly hot topic of discussion, being similar to thinking about your parents having sex.

However, the 1960s and especially the 1970s also saw a significant increase in the number of single women entering seminary who wished to become parish ministers. This was a startling occurrence to the centuries-old, male bastions of religious learning, many of which didn't have women's bathrooms in most buildings. (Some seminaries merely switched the sign on the men's room door from "Men" to "Women," without changing the plumbing inside.)

Another seismic shift also occurred about this time, when the United Church of Christ ordained its first gay minister in 1972. Overnight, the issue of clergy sexuality became a subject of discussion in congregational life, as increasing numbers of gays and lesbians perceived a call to ministry, completed seminary, went into search, found parishes to serve, and brought their same-sex partners with them.

Or, these gay and lesbian ministers came alone, sometimes "out of the closet" and sometimes not. Similar to the single, heterosexual, female pastor, gays and lesbians had not ruled out the prospect of finding a partner. These new arrivals signaled a momentous shift in American religion. Most American churchgoers had never encountered a single pastor, let alone one who would be involved in the dating scene, gay or straight.

In the late 1970s, HIV/AIDS made its frightening appearance, making matters of sexuality among both gay and straight people a worldwide concern, clergy included.

The issue of gay clergy reached an explosive moment in 2003, with the consecration of Eugene Robinson as the first openly gay bishop in the Episcopal Church. As a priest, Robinson had been in a heterosexual marriage for many years. He "came out" later in life, and lived openly with his male partner. Episcopal parishes across the nation experienced massive defections, as parishioners departed in anger. Robinson's ordination created a schism in the Worldwide Anglican Communion, and the unrest continues today.

In 2009, the Lutherans removed the requirement of celibacy for partnered gay clergy, but single clergy, gay or straight, are to remain celibate. Those ministers in partnership must maintain publicly accountable, lifelong, monogamous relationships. Whether gay or lesbian ministers in partnership will be called to a church remains another matter altogether. The Presbyterians followed suit in 2011, and the American Baptists maintain similar standards. These decisions required years of debate, much of it rancorous, and denominations have seen breakaway congregations and members leaving in large numbers.

But standards remain murky as to who is ordained and who can serve as clergy. In 2011, United Methodist Church minister Amy DeLong was charged with two violations of the Book of Discipline. The first was for being a "self avowed practicing homosexual" even though the bishop was well aware of her sexual orientation when she was appointed as a parish minister. The second was for conducting a same-sex wedding ceremony. She was found not guilty on the first count, and guilty on the second.

In 2012, the highest court in the Presbyterian Church (USA) upheld the censure of Rev. Jane Spahr for performing sixteen same-gender marriages in California during a period when such marriages were legal in the state.

Federal employment laws also changed, with the Supreme Court decision in 2012 involving the case of Hosanna-Tabor Evangelical Lutheran Church and School vs. Equal Employment Opportunity Commission. The court ruled that religious bodies have the power to decide which individuals will minister to the faithful, a doctrine known as "ministerial exception." It remains unclear how this ruling will play out regarding gay or lesbian clergy.

Your own church

Early in the search process, congregations and search committees alike need to determine whether they will interview gay or lesbian clergy. Some congregations are "open and affirming" while others in that same faith tradition are not. Decisions tend to be based on a congregation's theology and geographic location. For instance, you're not likely to find a lot of gay clergy in churches below the Mason-Dixon line, but you will in Boston, New York, Chicago, and Washington, DC.

As previously noted, judicatories sometimes serve as gatekeepers, and refer the names of ministerial candidates to churches in their regions. Some churches are on record that they will not consider a gay pastor, and these wishes are respected. Other judicatories disregard this request, believing their role is not to pass judgment on candidates.

Judicatories and search committees alike surely realize that single male and female ministers do not always reveal their sexual orientation, whether gay or straight. Thus, it may be difficult for a judicatory official or a search committee to determine the sexual preference of the single minister.

To delve into the subject of changing clergy families today, whatever their sexual orientation and their chances of being called to a parish, we need explore the issues of clergy families and changing norms a bit further. The traditional married, heterosexual clergy couple is as good a place to begin as any, so let's pull back the veil and see what we find.

Dating, sex, and the clergy family

Even today, there remains a subtle but lingering belief among people of many faith traditions that ordination and sexuality do not go together. Someone who is spiritual should not be sexual, and congregants often desire clergy whose sexuality is not obvious or apparent. Due in part to monastic orders, holy people are often viewed as celibate. In fact, one argument against ordaining women was the presence of female bodies would create lust in their male counterparts.[2]

Church members wish to perceive their ministers as moral exemplars, especially in smaller communities where the pastor is a visible part of civic life. As God's representative on earth, clergy demonstrate this by their daily behavior. Most lay people expect clergy to exemplify and display all Christian virtues at all times. The minister's wife may take her husband's arm as they stroll along, but signs of overt affection (and thus, potential sexuality) are frowned upon.

Straight clergy

Remaining on the heterosexual side of the fence, we have the aforementioned married couple, with or without children. But the clergy family today may include birth children and adopted children, some of a different race. A Caucasian minister and her Caucasian husband might show up with an Asian child and an African- American child. Clergy families also now include both husbands and wives in second marriages and their "blended families," children from both previous marriages.

Speaking of children, the married couple who gives birth to children while serving a congregation is a wondrous thing to behold, creating great joy and delight. But I once overheard a parishioner say of the new female pastor, "She'd better not get pregnant. She's here to take care of us!"

Next on the list, we have the divorced straight minister, male or female, perhaps with children, perhaps without. We can add to the mix whether that single male or female minister will be dating. Here, unfortunately, sexist attitudes remain strongly in place. Single clergy find it more difficult to be settled in a new parish than married clergy, and female clergy serve smaller parishes and are paid less than their male colleagues.

Congregations are sometimes wary of divorced or single female clergy because the unattached minister, especially if she is attractive, may be viewed as a sexualized minister. This is more so for women than men. Few congregants relish the idea of their female minister dating a number of men, let alone sleeping with them. Better that she devote more time to her parish work.

For the single male minister, it is just the opposite. Parishioners don't want the pastor to be lonely, and it's assumed that he will marry again. In fact, Harry's cousin Angela might be the perfect woman. Maybe we should arrange an introduction.

Parishioners are less likely to arrange blind dates for the female pastor. As for gay and lesbian clergy, most parishioners do not have a large circle of gay friends and probably aren't in the matchmaking business, though I'm sure there have been exceptions.

As for dating a minister, women supposedly find male ministers attractive because they are perceived as being thoughtful and caring. In stark contrast, men can find female ministers threatening because they are intelligent, hold leadership roles, and are supposed to be holy in all things. Hitting on a female minister? Isn't that off-limits?

Speaking of off-limits, there's also the issue of whether the single pastor, male or female, gay or straight, will date parishioners. Some denominations strictly prohibit single clergy dating parishioners. Other denominations recommend that parishioners who date the minister find a new parish. Standards vary, but are usually discussed with ministers in regard to boundary issues.

I don't wish to portray people in the pews as complete prudes. Author Allison Moore writes of a single, female pastor who saw the return of an old flame who wanted to reconnect. The romance flourished, much to the congregation's delight, and a few years later, the entire congregation was invited to the wedding. The women of the parish held a bridal shower, and with great joy recounted how they told the sales clerk that the sexy underwear they were buying was for their priest![3]

Finally, on the subject of straight clergy, a denominational official recently told me about two ministers in similar situations. The first was a male minister who was being considered as associate pastor in a multi-staff church. He told the search committee that he was in a committed relationship with a woman, but they were not ready to be married. If he was called, she would come with him and they would live together. The church leadership considered the issue, and gave him the okay.

The other case was a woman being considered as sole pastor. She told the search committee that she was in a committed relationship with a man, but they were not ready to marry. If called, he would come along and they would live together. After some discussion, the leadership of the church said they could not in good conscience approve her living arrangement.

Double standards exist, which brings us back to gay and lesbian clergy.

Gay and lesbian couples and families

"The constant need for GLBT people to justify their own existence and full humanity, or to hear their lives discussed as an object of debate, or to deny an essential part of themselves in order to be accepted, take a costly toll on their lives and on the church as a whole."[4]

Whether gay clergy in search are "out" or not seems to encompass a number of beliefs. The first is that straight pastors have an edge over gay pastors, with the former having greater odds of being called to a new parish. Thus, gay clergy may adopt a, "Don't ask, don't tell" attitude.

Gay clergy going this route may believe that sexual preference isn't a factor in effective ministry, and they can function just fine without ever bringing up the subject. I know a number of single pastors who have served their parishes successfully for twenty years or more who fit this description, and in fact, I'm unsure of their sexual orientation.

Some gay clergy believe they might eventually reveal their true identities over time, as they become established in their ministry. I recall one pastor who had a very youthful look about him. When he gave his "coming out" sermon, he mentioned that he would soon be forty and it was time to be honest about who he was. During the coffee hour, a number of parishioners remarked, "I didn't know the pastor was that old!" Most parishioners suspected he was gay, and his admitted sexual orientation barely registered on the congregational meter.

In contrast, gay clergy who self-identify believe they need to be forthright while in search. In being open, they realize the risks of being passed by all too well, often by ministers with less experience. One issue that search committees seem to be concerned about is a gay minister who comes "with an agenda." This agenda seems to be framing the entirety of his or her ministry through the lens of gay rights. One gay minister I spoke with said he's definitely in the open about his sexual orientation, but he's not "in your face" about it.

Issues of the gay minister extend beyond the search and call. A United Church of Christ minister I spoke with was open during the search, and called to a parish. He was informed afterwards that seven families left the church before they even met him. This was a very painful experience, to be judged in absentia.

Legal or not?

In some states, same-sex marriage is legal, while in other states, it's not. Yet other states have approved civil unions. Thus, in some churches, a gay or lesbian minister has a spouse in marriage; while in other churches, perhaps fifty miles down the road and across a state border, that same couple would be living without benefit of legal marriage.

All these issue swirling around brings us, in my view, to a hopeful conclusion. It's not about who's doing what to whom, but rather the quality of loving and caring relationships that clergy and congregants alike strive to achieve.

Concluding remarks

I've quoted minister and author Allison Moore a number of times, and it seems fitting to end with one last reference from her work.

"All denominations expect clergy and their families, when they have families, to live in accordance with Scripture and Christian tradition. My view includes the broadest vision of Christian families –

heterosexual couples and same-sex couples, single mothers raising children, biological and adopted children, and so on, all of whom are clear that God has blessed their families."[5]

To which I say, "Amen, sister!" But churchgoers need to be cognizant of older members who grew up in very different times. A friend of mine is 84 years old, and attended a private women's college in New England, which remains single-sex to this day. In her era, a gentleman caller was introduced to the dorm mother and chatted with her in the parlor, the only area in the dormitory a man was permitted, while the young woman was summoned. Today, on that same campus, men can live in their girl-friend's dorm room for weeks at a time.

In mainline churches, the older the parishioners, the less they may accept a minister or clergy family that falls outside traditional definitions. At the same time, it's possible that older generations have gay children or grandchildren, or heterosexual grandkids who are cohabiting without benefit of clergy. Older generations may not approve of this, and may never approve. Well into the 1970s, a divorced minister was a scorned minister whose service to the church was over and done with forever. Times do indeed change.

Younger generations are considerably more tolerant, thankfully, and issues of sexual orientation and cohabitation are commonplace. It's just "no big deal" they tell me nonchalantly. Every generation creates anew, and with the passage of time, the clergy family, in all its wondrous possi-bilities, will enrich and enhance the church and all our lives.

References

Introduction

1. Adair Lammis, *What Do Lay People Want in Pastoral Leadership?* Duke University, Pulpit and Pew Research on Pastoral Leadership, 2003. 21.

Chapter One

1. Adair Lammis, What Do Lay People Want in Pastoral Leadership? 42.

Chapter Two

1. Joseph Umidi, *Confirming the Pastoral Call* (Grand Rapids, MI: Kregel Publications, 2000), 53.

2. Peter Raible, *How to Case a Church*, Self-published manuscript, 1985, 29.

3. James M. Antal, *Considering a New Call: Ethical and Spiritual Challenges for Clergy* (Herndon, VA: The Alban Institute, 2000), Preface.

4. Barbara Melosh, "You Are Not Equipped," *Christian Century Magazine*, May 4, 2010, page 28.

5. John Kotter, "How to Save Good Ideas," *Harvard Business Review*, October, 2010, pp 129-132.

6. Thom S. Rainier and Eric Geiger, *Simple Church* (Nashville, TN: B & H Publishing, 2006), 22-23.

7. Anthony Pappas, in *Pastor Search*, 42.

8. Barbara Brown Taylor, *Leaving Church* (San Francisco, CA: Harper, 2006), 155-66.

9. Paul Nixon, *I Refuse to Lead a Dying Church* (Cleveland, OH: Pilgrim Press, 2006), 18.

10. Carolyn Weese and J. Russell Crabtree, *The Elephant in the Boardroom* (San Francisco, CA: Jossey Bass Publishers, 2004), 106.

Chapter Three

1. Lyle Schaller, *Discontinuity and Hope: Radical Change and the Path to the Future* (Nashville, TN. Abingdon Press, 1999), 27.

2. Miroslav Volf, "Way of Life," in *Christian Century Magazine*, November 20 – December 3, 2002. 35.

Chapter Four

1. Loren Mead, *A Change of Pastors* (Herndon, VA: The Alban Institute, 2005), 22.

2. Pat Jobe, *365 Ways to Criticize the Preacher* (Macon, GA: Smyth & Hedways Publishing, Inc. 2002), 2.

3. Weese and Crabtree, *The Elephant in the Boardroom*, 60.

4. Weston Gentry, "Faith and Cowboys", *The Denver Post*, January 22, 2012, 1B.

5. George Barna, *Futurecast* (Austin, TX: Tyndale House Publishers, 2011), 123-200.

6. Bruce Robison, "We Can Do This," *The Living Church Magazine*, Jan 1, 2012, 21.

Chapter Six

1. Loren Mead, *A Change of Pastors*, 2.

2. Joseph Umidi, *Confirming the Pastoral Call*, 18.

3. Loren Mead, *A Change of Pastors*, 76

4. Paul Nixon, *I Refuse to Lead a Dying Church*, 57.

5. Arlen J. Rothauge, *Sizing Up a Congregation* (New York: Episcopal Church Center), 13-20.

6. Isaac S. Villegas, "Organizing for Communion," *Christian Century Magazine,* March 21, 2012, 26.

7. Megan McArdle, "Why Companies Fail," *The Atlantic Magazine,* March, 2012, 28-32.

Chapter Seven

1. Weese and Crabtree, *The Elephant in the Boardroom,* 131.

2. Lyle Schaller, *44 Steps Up Off the Plateau* (Nashville, TN: Abingdon Press, 1999), 193.

Chapter Eight

1. Joseph Umidi, *Confirming the Pastoral Call,* 27.

2. Weese and Crabtree, *The Elephant in the Boardroom,* 30.

3. Bunty Ketchum, *So You're on the Search Committee* (Herndon, VA: The Alban Institute, 2005), 10.

4. Riley Walker and Marcia Patton, *When the Spirit Moves: A Guide for Ministers in Transition.* (Valley Forge, PA: Judson Press, 2011), 92.

5. Loren Mead, *A Change of Pastors,* 49.

6. Joseph Umidi, *Confirming the Pastoral Call,*14.

7. Dean E. Foos, *Searching for a Pastor the Presbyterian Way* (Louisville, KY, Geneva Press, 2001), 78.

8. Weese and Crabtree, *The Elephant in the Boardroom,* 33.

Chapter Nine

1. Riley Walker and Marcia Patton, *When the Sprit Moves,* 28.

2. Edward Hammett, *Reaching People Under 40 While Keeping People over 60* (St. Louis, MO: Chalice Press, 2007), 88.

3. Joseph Umidi, *Confirming the Pastoral Call,* 33.

4. Christopher C. Moore, *Opening the Clergy Parachute* (Nashville, TN: Abingdon Press, 1995), 36.

5. Louis McBurney, *Every Pastor Needs a Pastor*, (Waco, TX: Word Press, 1977)

Chapter Ten

1. Ashley Hale, *The Lost Art of Church Fundraising* (Chicago, IL: Precept Press, 1993), 78.

2. Peter Raible, *How to Case a Church*, 16.

3. Robert Wuthnow, *The Crisis in the Churches: Spiritual Malaise, Fiscal Woe* (New York, NY: Oxford University Press, 1999), 230.

Chapter Eleven

1. Aubrey Malphurs, *Leading Leaders: Empowering Church Boards for Ministry Excellence* (Grand Rapids, MI: Baker Books, 2005), 17-18, 61.

2. Lyle Schaller, *Create Your Own Future* (Nashville, TN: Abingdon Press, 1991), 31.

3. Edwin Friedman, *A Failure of Nerve: Leadership in the Age of the Quick Fix* (Bethesda, MD: The Edwin Friedman Estate/Trust, 1999),11.

4. Anthony Robinson, "How to Follow the Leader," *Christian Century Magazine,* January 11, 2012, 31.

5. Robert K. Greenleaf, *Servant Leadership: A Journey into the Nature of Legitimate Power and Greatness* (New York, NY: Paulist Press, 1977), 28-29.

6. Richard Lischer, *Open Secrets: A Spiritual Journey Through a Country Church* (New York, NY: Random House, 2001), 56.

7. Patton and Walker, *When the Spirit Moves,* 101.

Chapter Twelve

1. Charles Merrill Smith, *How to Become a Bishop Without Being Religious* (New York, NY: Doubleday and Company, 1965), 19-28.

2. Allison A. Moore, *Clergy Moms* (New York, NY: Seabury Books, 2008), 64.

3. Allison A. Moore, *Clergy Moms*, 82.

4. Allison A. Moore, *Clergy Moms*, 20.

5. Allison A. Moore, *Clergy Moms*, 133.